CHILDREN'S MEDIA YEARBOOK 2015

The Children's Media Yearbook is a publication of The Children's Media Foundation

Director, Greg Childs
Administrator, Jacqui Wells

The Children's Media Foundation
P.O. Box 56614
London W13 0XS

info@thechildrensmediafoundation.org

First published 2015

ISBN 978-0-9575518-4-8

Book and cover design by Jack Noel

CHILDREN'S MEDIA YEARBOOK 2015

EDITED BY

LYNN WHITAKER & **BETH HEWITT**

The Children's Media
FOUNDATION

EDITORIAL

LYNN WHITAKER AND BETH HEWITT

Hello and welcome to another issue of The Children's Media Yearbook. 2015 is our third year of publication and whether you are new to the yearbook or familiar with its ambit, we are confident that you will enjoy the diverse perspectives that it offers on a wide range of children's media topics. Published by the Children's Media Foundation (CMF), a not-for-profit body now firmly established as the leading UK advocacy body for quality and choice in children's media, the yearbook serves to inform and stimulate reasoned debate across the issues – whether of policy, production and audience – that are relevant to children's media. It also acts as a record of the changing mood of the times, particularly when taking a longitudinal view of how industry responds to the needs of the audience and the impact of policy. No other publication attempts this and, given the often ephemeral nature of children's media and its discourses, it's really useful to have a book that captures the flavour of what was floating our boat or exercising our spleen each year. As such it is an ambitious but rewarding undertaking, of ongoing value to parents, researchers and producers alike.

There is more – much more, as there is much to tell – on the work of the CMF in this introductory section, as Director, Greg Childs, offers a round-up of achievements in the last three years. This is then followed by a piece from a new 'Founder Patron', Lady Rabia Abdul-Hakim, who argues for greater diversity in the aspirational characters created in children's media, telling a damn good yarn along the way of how she came to be a children's media creator and why she believes the work of CMF to be so important. As ever we stress that the views represented in the yearbook are that of the individual authors and the editors too are independent. The yearbook then does not reflect the views of CMF as an organisation but, instead, fits with the avowed aim of encouraging discussion around those viewpoints.

Each year the yearbook content is commissioned (we are good at arm-twisting!) in such a way as to present a range of perspectives and it is always fascinating how particular themes emerge across the book as a whole. We make no apologies for kicking off this year's volume with an entire section devoted to 'Children's Public Service Broadcasting' (PSB) - in the UK and beyond

- but we hadn't really foreseen the extent to which the threads of PSB discourse can be seen throughout *all* sections of the book. Perhaps, as we gear up for the process of BBC charter renewal – and its attendant focus on the licence fee – we shouldn't be surprised that questions of commissioning, funding and policy run deep through the book, given the centrality of the BBC as a champion of children's content.

Alice Webb, brand new Director of BBC Children's, makes no apologies whatsoever for lauding the BBC's achievements for children, and wants to ensure BBC Children's remains, "Pioneering, unforgettable, and a part of the rich heritage that's shaped our lives and will shape the lives of today's British kids too." Jeanette Steemers follows on then, in her article, to argue that children's content is crucial to the mission of *any* public service broadcaster and points to the challenges and threats to that mission, not just in the UK, but globally. Alice and Jeanette's contributions help to frame the themes of the five remaining articles in the section, in which models and aspirations of children's public service media are reflected on in Poland (Agnieszka Weglinska), New Zealand (Ruth Zanker), Canada

(Natalie Coulter and Kerrie-Ann Bernard), Japan (Sachiko Kodaira) and the US (Russell Miller).

Our next section, 'Industry Reflections and Debates', critiques the current trends in media production and content and explores the real life themes and issues that confront the producers of animation and children's production in 2015. Andy Robertson begins by exploring the 'toys-to-life' genre, a concept that takes its audience back to the world of physical toys whilst skilfully combining it with games, apps and on-screen characters. Dan Bays and Jon Haywood take us on a journey into the magical world of all things digital and look at the rapidly changing landscape from inside the BBC, with the spotlight on Childrens as the leader of this brave new world.

So, we might consider *everything* to be digital now, but what about the history of how we have arrived at this place? The remaining articles in the section deal in different ways with history, heritage and transition. In his personal account of running an animation company, Ken Anderson adeptly navigates the policy rollercoaster: with its twists and turns, with its supporters and the people at the top realigning tax breaks and incentives, with, as always, the financial stability of animation and children's media production relying on those vagaries. It's a must read for all those hoping against hope that support is around the corner. Next up, Michael Algar provides a potted history of how the animation sector in Ireland has been supported and outlines the work of Animation Ireland. The article serves as both a history and a 'how to', again outlining, this time from an Irish perspective, how creative industries policy plays out in practice.

Nostalgia has always been a part of the media industry and Peter Saunders's look back at animation in the North West of England could easily have fallen into this trap. Instead, it is a wholly pertinent and contemporary look at why the North West currently boasts so many innovative animation production companies. It's certainly a new dawn, against the odds maybe, but rooted in a creativity and passion for animation. In discussing the responsibilities of curation and heritage in children's content, Helen Wheatley critiques the nostalgia of children's television and the revival of the likes of *The Clangers* and *Teletubbies*, considering the importance of content which provides

cross-generational interaction as helpful in "reactivating a common culture of television that contemporary broadcasters often struggle to create in an era of niche programming and extensive choice". But, "Is that all there is?" asks Simon Parsons, in his essay recounting the birth of *Teacup Travels* with Great Aunt Lizzie and two young children, born digital: both in the show and in the article, nostalgia and the brave new digital world collide and bounce off each other, taking us all into the unknown. So the mantra is digital, the world is digital, but nostalgia for the past rates high on the clap-o-meter and whether in spite of or because of policy, children's media appears to be very much alive and kicking.

The third substantive section, 'Child and Youth Perspectives and Research', opens with Alison Preston's annual update on Ofcom's research with children, followed by Jenny Ehren's overview of the Childwise monitor data. While coming from different angles, both research pieces shed light on the digital trends and experiences of children and reveal much about children's (sometimes flawed) understanding of a crowded media landscape. We've deliberately set those research articles as an introduction to the

five contributions that follow, in which young people reflect on their own experiences, 'growing up digital'. It's the first time we've included the direct voice of children and young people in the yearbook and we're delighted to be able to do so, thanks to articles from Sophie Edwards, Josie Kelly, Flora Wilson Brown, Megan Nicholson and John Chisham. Their reflections range from nonplussed to cynical, and each is, by turns, fascinating, often amusing, and sometimes unsettling: together they suggest a definite generational zeitgeist. Following on from those pieces we grapple with the tricky questions of how to represent the experiences of children and youth and how to address the audience and create content that is enriching and meaningful. Cat Lewis's powerful account of making the documentary 'I Am Leo', and Angela Salt's hilarious yet poignant article on digging deep when writing comedy for children surely stand as examples of best practice in representing and addressing children through media.

Finally, as always, our yearbook closes with a 'Farewell' section in which we remember leading lights of children's media and reflect on programmes and institutions now past. Katy Jones, Terry Pratchett and Terry

Sue-Patt are all remembered here - in thoughtful reflection and tribute by Barney Harwood, Ann Giles and Phil Redmond respectively – and then, perhaps with a playful tinge of irony, Jeremy Swan presents his invited retrospective of the fabulous *Rentaghost* as we continue our series of looking back at classic children's programmes of yesteryear. But we couldn't quite finish there, because, in an issue that raises so many questions about the future of children's public service media, we wanted to give the last word to someone who is uniquely placed to reflect on that and so we close on an 'Afterword' from Joe Godwin.

As ever, ALL our contributors give their articles for free (and we mustn't forget illustrations contributed by Stu Harrison and Chris Riddell) and that generosity of spirit speaks as much as anything for the passion and engagement that characterises the world of children's media and accords with the ethos of the yearbook; you can read all the biographies in the 'Contributors' section. For Lynn Whitaker this is her last year as editor and she wishes to express her thanks to all the contributors over the three issues. But rest assured plans are already underway for the 2016 issue and Beth Hewitt will be there to ensure continuity for the incoming editor. So – as ever – keep the ideas coming!

THE CHILDREN'S MEDIA FOUNDATION: THE FIRST THREE YEARS

GREG CHILDS

The Children's Media Foundation was first conceived by Anna Home in late 2011 and was launched in January 2012 as an amalgamation of Save Kids' TV and the Children's Film and Television Foundation (CFTF).

Save Kids' TV had spent five years campaigning for additional funding for children's television in the UK, as a reaction to the collapse in commissioning by the commercial public service broadcasters like ITV, and had success in at least achieving awareness of the problems amongst politicians, civil servants and the regulator, Ofcom. The CFTF was itself the successor to the Children's Film Foundation (CFF), set up in the 1950s to support the children's film industry in the UK using 'Eady Levy' money - a small tax on every cinema ticket sold - designed to stimulate the production of British films. A considerable number of kids' features were made and shown to enthusiastic audiences at Saturday morning screenings. They still have an audience today in a series of DVDs issued by the British Film Institute, which looks after the CFF archive.

The aims of the new organisation were:

- To continue campaigning for plurality of supply, quality, variety and UK-relevance in children's media of all kinds, on all platforms.
- To establish new relationships between the academic research community and the industry - and to bring research to politicians , policy-makers and parents – in order to build a more reasoned approach to policy-making and to improve media literacy amongst parents and children. Basically, to create more 'informed' policy and a more media literate audience, better able to cope with the rapid changes in content, distribution and consumption that we face in the modern media landscape.
- To preserve and promote the archive and the traditions of quality in children's media production - looking back to look forward - maintaining the best of the past to inform future thinking.

I took on the role of Director midway through the first year, tasked with developing a stable and respected organisation which could address the above with confidence and broad support. It was decided not to become an industry body, but instead to be a 'critical friend' to children's media-makers and the platforms where content is carried. Since the outset the Foundation has always put first the best interests of the *audience* in all its dealings with the industry, and in the political sphere.

To achieve that stability, funding was an immediate issue for the CMF. It was decided to approach this through a system of donations, and it has to be admitted this has been a story of slow growth. The CMF still relies on the annual donations of its supporters and patrons; the larger contributions of the growing number of 'Founder Patrons' who make a lifetime donation; the support of various like-minded organisations such as guilds and associations; and, most recently, the corporate support of companies, big and small, working in the children's media sector, who see what we do as crucial to the continued health of the industry. I'll admit that funding has proved more difficult to raise than we hoped (though perhaps at least as difficult as we expected). As we go into our fourth year we are beginning to see progress though and if we can now build on that momentum we will reach a more assured financial status that will allow the Foundation to do more and achieve more. That, of course, depends on our supporters continuing to come onside and offer their active backing - as individuals or companies - if we are to survive and thrive.

That said, we have achieved much already. From the start Jayne Kirkham's dogged determination to give us (and the issues) a voice in Parliament has been one of our success stories. The All Party Parliamentary Group (APPG) for Children's Media and the Arts, under the Chairmanship of Baroness Benjamin (Floella to her fans and her friends in the industry), has continued to inform MPs and Peers as to what is actually happening in kids' media and in kids' media lives. It has brought researchers to the Houses of Parliament, along with industry specialists and activists, in respect of a number of areas, including the animation tax incentive campaign; children's working time regulations; and the responsibilities of online platform operators to children. The APPG has stimulated the attention of legislators regarding these issues and more, and, in one case, legislation within the Children's and Families Act has been the result.

Beyond that, our lobbying continues to bring these matters to the attention of ministers and shadow minsters, and Parliamentary Select Committees, with real impact. This includes the development of the new children's television tax incentive that we supported some years back as a partial solution to the continuing funding problems in children's TV commissioning. We were able to wholeheartedly support the producers association, PACT, on cultural grounds when they developed their specific and eventually successful campaign.

The idea that kids deserve access to their own culture - to hear their own voices; experience their own stories; and see the places they live - underpins everything we do. We want UK kids to have the richest possible media diet, with quality content coming from every corner of the world - particularly their own. So we've worked in the public space to respond to Ofcom's various analyses of the future of content delivery in the UK and to push for greater care and attention to the children's audience in the development of media policies in government: whether it be in considering the health of children's output at the BBC and the future of its funding and status; or how public service broadcasting is going to be regulated in the years ahead. Equally we have developed our relationships with regulators like Ofcom, the BBFC, the BBC Trust and the Office of Fair

Trading (now the Competition and Markets Authority) to offer ideas, connections to expertise, and a specific children's perspective into their wider thinking. Some examples of successful collaborations include a research-led consultation process with the OFT on their development of games industry guidelines for 'in-app purchasing' and a continuing contribution to Ofcom's research agenda amongst the younger audience and families.

Research has proved a fruitful area for CMF in general. We have launched the first iteration of Parent Portal, a web service which interprets academic research to answer parents' frequently asked questions about their children's media; and, more recently, the CMF Research Blog, which is a community of academics and researchers from diverse fields, interested in different aspects of media and children, that come together to 'compare notes'.

We have staged a number of events in the last three years and are building an ambitious programme for more. They range from policy-based discussions that have politicians in attendance, to issue-based creative conversations with industry practitioners. For the last three years, the CMF has

also been represented at the premier event of the children's media industry – the Children's Media Conference in Sheffield. Through sponsoring and producing sessions on a range of topics, we have captured the attention of the industry as the leaders in thinking on policy issues. We have also staged a delightful event which celebrated British preschool excellence while bringing together over 150 past presenters, musicians and production personnel from the much-loved *Play School* on its 50th anniversary.

Looking to the future, we plan to campaign vigorously to support the BBC Licence Fee, and to press for more regulation in commercial public service broadcasting, allied with a new 'contestable fund' to encourage broadcasters to produce more homegrown drama and factual programmes for children of all ages. We are exploring the rights children can expect online and the responsibilities service providers should fulfil to protect them. We'll be marking the 50th anniversary of *Jackanory* - later in 2015 - as a celebration of great British storytelling. And we are already planning the *Children's Media Yearbook* 2016.

And, in listing the achievements of the last three

years, CMF is proud to be the publisher of the *Children's Media Yearbook*. Lynn Whitaker has performed an amazing job as Yearbook editor for the first three editions: creating the concept from scratch; navigating the complexities of print-on-demand and Amazon and ITunes distribution; and commissioning the content, design and layout of what has became a much awaited and appreciated record of the children's media story, year by year, with the players, companies, personalities, challenges and triumphs all captured in one place – and a really good read!

My thanks to Lynn - who is now handing over the Editorship with the help of Beth Hewitt to smooth that transition - and to all the Executive Committee and Board members who have made so much happen in so short a time. Thanks too, to the supporters and patrons who have made the donations which make it all possible – we need more of you! With regular funding we can grow the CMF from this initial phase into an even more confident organisation.

Please help us to help children's media in the UK be the best that it can be for our kids. ☺

NEW HEROES WANTED: CREATING CULTURALLY-INSPIRED MEDIA

LADY RABIA ABDUL-HAKIM

Almost all great adventure stories start with these elements: a prophecy, a warrior, a mission and a weapon.

My story started just... like... that.

It was June, 1977. It was the summer before I started school, the summer before my fifth birthday. That was when my father told me something that would change the rest of my life. Excited, but worried about going to primary school in the fall, he had knelt down in front of me and stared into my huge eyes.

"If anyone bothers you, just poke 'um in the eyes like this," he said. Then, he made a 'V' with his fingers and jabbed forward at the air.

I smiled and nodded, enthusiastically.

He smiled then too, squeezed my shoulders and said, "Yeah, you're going be fine. You're a little warrior."

A few days later, he drowned.

And even as I watched them lower the brown casket into the grave with my mother's cries rising up to the sky like broken music chords, I decided I would be fine.

I had become a warrior and my father's words had become law.

As stories go, my weapons were initially absent. There was no TV when I was growing up in the Cayman Islands in the 1970s. So, we were encouraged to play, to draw and to read. All these things would eventually contribute to my arsenal of creativity.

My grandfather, who had to forgo his education to become a seaman aged thirteen, always ensured that I was amply supplied with bags of comics and mystery books like *Nancy Drew* and *The Hardy Boys*. At school, we were given *Dick & Jane* books. Some of you might remember those. They went like this, "See Jane run. See Dick run." I just wanted Dick and Jane to run away. Or do something fun like I did: play with rock babies, climb tamarind trees or tease Granny until she chased us.

I decided then that I wanted to be a writer when I grew up and write REALLY exciting stories. Funny stories. Scary stories. All kinds of stories. But most of all, stories with characters like me in them – stories with ethnic characters that had universal appeal. My mission was mapped.

By the time my grandfather brought the massive satellite dish and cemented it into the backyard, I already had a plethora of imaginary friends (characters) swarming through my mind. Still, nothing could have prepared me for the power of those Saturday morning cartoons. My sisters and I would have given up almost anything to watch the Smurfs trump Gargamel.

In fact, it was because of the (truly outrageous) Sunday morning scheduling of *Jem and the Holograms* that I boldly announced that we were abandoning Sunday school. For some odd reason, my mother did not react with the usual litany of admonitions. As I stood there with my arms daringly folded across my chest and my feet shoulder-width apart, she just stared at me, and then walked away, seeming to accept that we were damned. Braids bouncing, grinning and barefooted, I had ran to tell my sister that Jem had triumphed over Sunday school. And damned or not, we were elated.

After that, through rain or hurricane force winds, we jubilantly ran to the backyard to crank that Goliath satellite dish from one satellite after another. Yes, I was completely enthralled by those cartoons, by the music, the facial expressions, the slapstick comedy, the racing and jeering, and that bold, black outline around brilliant colour. But I was not alone: those cartoons enticed ALL the children in the neighbourhood. One by one they would quietly open the screen door, while gazing blankly at the TV, and sit cross-legged on the floor of my grandmother's porch, completely bewitched. Those cartoons captivated our attention and wielded enormous influence over us. We wanted every toy that was advertised and every character-laden cereal had to be breakfast: they were our Pied Piper and we were willingly mesmerized.

I slowly realized that I, too, had to access this powerful tool to empower my mission. I did this by drawing the characters that were swarming in my brain and documenting their stories, conceptualizing my media with a burgeoning imagination and a mere pencil and paper.

My weapons had appeared.

As I grew up, my mission ballooned into a magnificent obsession to promote the richness and enchantment of cultural diversity. I planned to do this by building a global, multicultural media company. And I promised my children that this company would be a legacy for them, and children all over the world. Little did I know that my dream would come at a price or that that little girl warrior would be in for the biggest battle of her life.

My story would span continents and exotic lands. It was the stuff legends are made of. In the end, I literally risked my life to fulfill that promise to my children. But finally, after fifteen years of countless setbacks, and against overwhelming odds, I did just that.

In August 2011, I launched, *Kaa Kaa and Tokyo*, the first culturally-inspired children's brand from the Cayman Islands, created with a singular purpose: to 'edutain'; to encourage children to read more; to read for pleasure; and to educate them about our culture and heritage. I now have other brands in development.

Moving to the UK in June 2014, and becoming a Patron of CMF, accords with the success of my mission. The CMF is dedicated to quality in children's media through diversity and choice and brings together a network of stakeholders united in the belief that children's media *matters*; that children deserve the best quality across all platforms; and that decisions affecting children's media should always have a sound evidence base. The knowledge and experience contained in CMF – connecting audience, industry, research and policy - is priceless and I can benefit from that wisdom. But it's not about my benefit: above all it's about the audience. The audience needs a champion and someone who can advocate on their behalf to help inform policy decisions.

And we need heroes that truly reflect the UK's pluralistic society. Though the diversity issue is being addressed regarding gender and sexuality, I assert that additional multicultural media is vital, given the global problems caused by racism, extremism and intolerance. We need multicultural heroes with inspiring, universally appealing stories; because appreciating our differences and recognizing our similarities, will enrich our communities and our economy. Broadcasters still defensively assert that multicultural children's media IS available. Yes, things have improved but I insist that in the UK more progress is still needed. Like Oliver Twist, I am calling for MORE new heroes.

I emphatically believe that multicultural children's media can be a critical tool for cultural diplomacy: inevitably promoting tolerance, intercultural dialogue and global peace.

One thing cannot be denied: the power of traditional media is dwindling. Media is no longer corporate-born or controlled. It is now being birthed by the audiences themselves, and socially and digitally distributed to the masses, in seconds. I think this trend will have an overwhelming positive impact for Black, Asian, Minority and Ethnic (BAME) audiences. Undoubtedly, with the rise of self-publishing and easy access digital platforms, other multicultural creators, like me, are feeling optimistic.

Yes, I do feel hopeful as I think about the little girl warrior running barefoot and I sketch yet another character. I create, represent, advocate and remain steadfast.

And so, the adventure continues… ◔

CHILDREN'S PUBLIC SERVICE BROADCASTING

BBC CHILDREN'S

ALICE WEBB

Simon Groom.

That's the answer to the one question I've been asked the most since taking on the role of Director of BBC Children's this March. And so ubiquitous is the BBC's homegrown children's TV, that most of you (well, if you're over 30) will instantly know the question.

I don't think I'll ever tire of answering it though - or any other question about my job for that matter. Because one of the great joys of being part of BBC Children's is the connection so many people of all ages have to it. Mention it to total strangers and their eyes light up as they start talking about *Play School*, *The Wombles*, Gordon the Gopher, *Blue Peter*, *Grange Hill* and a whole range of other shows and characters that have stayed with them for years.

Of course, this is evidence of what most of us know: BBC Children's is a great British institution, as iconic as Big Ben and just as much a part of our national consciousness. Pioneering, unforgettable, and a part of the rich heritage that's shaped our lives and will shape the lives of today's British kids too.

Or will it?

Utterly amazing

We've already established that I'm new to BBC Children's. So just this once, I'm going to take full advantage of being the new kid on the block and do some brazen promotion and lauding of what we do.

I think BBC Children's content is utterly amazing.

As the UK's main public service broadcaster, we're here to inform, educate, entertain and inspire all of the 9.3m children aged 0-12 in the UK today,[1] with high quality, U-rated brain food. And this ethos sets an unmistakable BBC Children's tone which, like the proverbial stick of rock, runs through everything we do – although a lot more nourishing for the consumer.

We offer children, their parents and anyone else who wants to engage with us - and they do in droves - the very best multi-genre, UK-originated TV, radio, games and apps. Content that's rooted in the real lives of British families and the communities they live in, and reflects them back to children in all their diverse and technicolour glory.

The creativity, care and intelligence that goes into

crafting our shows, apps and games is really awe inspiring. And so is the result: brilliant content that promotes a whole range of life skills from creativity to language; digital expression to innovation. We enable children to learn, participate, have fun, thrive and realise their full potential in the rapidly-evolving digital world around them.

Content with breadth, quality and depth

Sometimes we're educational – albeit never stuffy. Think about Dr Chris and Dr Xand teaching kids about what happens when they sneeze on *Operation Ouch*, or *Nina and the Neurons* using motion capture suits to explain to under-sixes how animation looks so realistic.

Sometimes we're challenging and we push boundaries. Think about CBBC's BAFTA-winning and critically acclaimed *My Life* documentaries. Like 'I am Leo', the first programme on children's TV to deal with transgender issues (Cat Lewis talks about making the documentary later in this yearbook), or *Poppy's Day*, a story read by Simon Weston on CBeebies Radio, which introduced the concept of war sensitively to our littlest audience using emotions such as bravery that they can understand.

Sometimes we're about having unadulterated fun and laughs, such as with Wigan's most irrepressible canine export, Hacker T Dog, or preschool comedy sketch show, *Gigglebiz*.

Sometimes we bring kids and parents together for noisy, bonkers, live-action, family fun - putting family members up to mischief in *Sam and Mark's Friday Wind-Up* or subjecting them to the pirate obstacle course in *Swashbuckle*.

Sometimes we're about sharing the big news stories and the hard facts of life. Think about *Newsround*'s moving report about Horace, the fourteen year old boy soldier from Leeds who was killed in the battle of the Somme after having lied about his age in order to fight in the war. Or 'Being Me', a *Newsround* special that deals with the complex issue of body image and how we see ourselves.

And, every single time, we're all about producing incredible content - whether inhouse, or with partners and a wealth of indies - content with a breadth, depth and quality that never ceases to amaze me.

Citizens of the future
In a sea of non-UK and non-public service channels and media, we offer an important and valuable alternative that looks to help build the citizens of the future. Not just out of duty, but because we're in the enviable position of being able to see that when we create content that inspires children it can truly shape positive lives. In turn, this inspires us to go further, think bigger, strive harder and challenge ourselves to break new boundaries. BBC Children's loves serving British kids in this way –

and we do it with a passion that burns as brightly today as it ever has.

For my part, it's a real privilege to be leading BBC Children's - not to mention a huge responsibility. As the custodian of this national treasure I am keenly aware of not just the brilliance of the content we offer children, but its precious value to the whole country, young and old alike.

The world is running fast – and we're on our toes ready to keep running with it
So I think we've established that I believe we do some great stuff for UK kids. It all sounds positive and perfect doesn't it? Well, yes actually. To some extent, it really is pretty perfect. I have to say that loudly and clearly because I'm in no doubt about how fortunate we are to be in a position to do the wondrous job we do. But it's not just a bowl of cherries.

We're all in the grip of the most exciting revolution seen for generations – the digital revolution. It's fundamental, fast moving and at the heart of our audience more than any other. It's changed the landscape beyond recognition already, challenging everything we do and raising some tough questions.

Like, how do we make sure we keep our curious and media-savvy audience with us when there are hundreds of alternatives across an ever-increasing range of platforms?

It's opening up opportunities like never before too: for example, our two YouTube channels give us the freedom and flexibility to react quickly to what's happening in the world and create the memes and clips we know our audience loves to share with each other. Just in the last few weeks, millions of people across the globe have heard the names CBBC and *Newsround*, as we reported on how Harry and Charlie (stars of 800m-times-viewed YouTube smash 'Charlie Bit My Finger'), now aged eleven and nine, feel about their infantile infamy. A wide range of international media outlets including *The Independent*, *The New York Post*, Buzzfeed, ABC News and E-Online reported on our clip and there have been over 2.1m views of the clip on our CBBC YouTube channel. Amazing.

But it's not just the digital revolution that's shaping the landscape of young lives in Britain today; just as it always has, the nature of childhood is evolving and this impacts on kids' lives too. Sociological, economic and global shifts have fundamentally altered the notion of family, childhood and community.

For example, we now have more diverse children and young people than ever before, with 78% of 0-12s from White British backgrounds and 22% from other ethnic groups.[2] And we know that the polarisation of lives and opportunities is especially pronounced among the 54% of kids living in ABC1 homes and 46% in C2DE homes today,[3] compared to some previous generations.

Given what we know about the powerful impact of socioeconomic status and parental engagement on, for example, children's literacy and numeracy,[4] we recognise the incredibly important role public service media plays in supporting learning and parenting in the home. That's why the CBeebies 'learning through play' ethos is so central to all of its content, and why we continue to prioritise education for kids as they grow up with us.

These factors may have been more gradual that the digital revolution, but are no less profound. Combined, these issues provide a challenge - exciting and daunting in equal measure – that all providers of children's media have to meet. And although the world is

moving fast, the great thing is that BBC Children's is match fit with plenty of energy and passion to keep moving with it.

BBC Children's was the first part of the BBC to offer connected, multiplatform content across our TV and online platforms. And we really have embraced it: later you

can take a look at the rather excellent article on interactive and digital frontiers, written by my colleagues Jon Howard and Daniel Bays, to find out just how (and yes, BBC Children's earns a proud shout out in *every* section of this yearbook).

Staying connected with the connected generation

Of course, we know we can't afford to stand still for a second in our quest to stay connected to the 'connected generation'. And there are some choices to make too, because creating the digital content kids love, and that works across many platforms, raises some really big issues.

Unlike linear TV content, which we finance up front and can be repeated, digital content needs to be constantly updated and invested in. And in a world of hungry young minds, infinite opportunities and myriad content platforms, can you guess what is very definitely not infinite? That's right, our funds. That's just one of the reality checks we're dealing with.

So how best to do we serve our children's audience in a fragmented digital world? Where do we focus our energies? Where do we place some bets? Those are just some of the questions I'll be looking into, with the BBC Children's team and our partners, over the coming months.

A world leader in our field

But back to the here and now.

BBC Children's is a globally unique proposition – truly a world leader in our field. How many other UK organisations can say that?

I've broken the habit of a lifetime to tell you, in this terribly un-British way, why I think we're utterly amazing in this article. And I've done that because, while we are great at making unique content that's worth the licence fee and fulfils a hugely important need in the UK, we Brits are not always great at claiming credit and shouting about it.

Of course, we don't do it by ourselves. What you see and hear on BBC TV and online platforms, made especially for UK children, is a result of the vibrant, creative and passionate partners, indies, inhouse production teams and talent we work with. We all share the same ambition: to inform, educate, entertain and inspire children to enjoy their childhood; to thrive in the world around them; and to realize their full potential into adulthood.

Don't get me wrong, I know we're not perfect. But it's good for all – the BBC, the children's media industry and our young audiences - for us to take a moment to remind ourselves and others just how special and rather wonderful BBC Children's is.

And here's how you can help. The BBC has recently launched a great campaign asking us all to let our love show for BBC programmes. You simply click on the heart button next to one of our shows on BBC iPlayer (on the grown-ups iPlayer site only, because our distinct CBeebies and CBBC iPlayer channels are 'walled gardens' to protect kids). It couldn't be simpler. And if you follow the link, you can see what everyone else loves too.

So if you think we're worth it and want to champion us too, love us with that heart button, show us you care and join us in talking about our unique and important purpose for today and the next generation – no matter how quickly things are moving! ⊙

1   BBC Audiences / BARB
2   BBC Audiences / BARB
3   BBC Audiences / BARB
4   Leon Feinstein (2003)

CHILDREN'S CONTENT – CRUCIAL FOR ANY PUBLIC SERVICE BROADCASTER

JEANETTE STEEMERS

Good entertaining children's content that is accessible on a variety of platforms is a really vital and essential component of public service broadcasting. And, in fact, when the BBC was campaigning for its charter renewal back in 1998, it produced a promotional video, 'Small People', showcasing a huge array of absolutely amazing children's programming produced inhouse and by independent producers, which reminded the public precisely of that: that the BBC has a long and rich history of making wonderful and memorable content for small people because of the "unique way it was paid for by big people".

If the BBC wants to appeal to future generations then this ability to call on our collective memory of inspiring programmes made by *both* the BBC and a diverse range of independent producers is crucial to its very survival. Yet BBC management rarely mention BBC Children's at all. This and some nagging concerns about the extent to which BBC Children's is working with larger transnational production companies on classic revivals (*Teletubbies, Danger Mouse*), combined with unanswered questions about where the production of children's content will sit once the rest of inhouse production is moved into a wholly-owned subsidiary, suggest that the BBC needs to take much greater care of its mission to serve children.

Quite apart from this the Corporation is missing a fantastic opportunity to connect with parents, politicians and the public in showing just how important it really is: because if the BBC fails to appeal to future generations *now*, it will surely atrophy over time as the public lose those fond memories: memories which the BBC has to work much harder to generate, because children have so many other opportunities in a fast changing media landscape. This is where the BBC has to show that it is both distinctive and popular in fulfilling its public service mission. Everyone recognises that it needs to work closely with the independent sector; but it also needs to ensure that there is some distance from the commercial objectives of its partners if it is to maintain the trust of parents and children.

Just how important children's content is for generating social cohesion and a sense of identity was clearly demonstrated to me and my colleague, Naomi Sakr, when we ran a workshop on 'Children's Content at the Core of Public Service Media in a Multiplatform Era' at the World Summit on Media for Children (WSMC), in Kuala Lumpur, Malaysia in September 2014 on behalf of the Commonwealth Broadcasting Association (now Public Media Alliance). With 40 participants from twenty different countries ranging from Afghanistan to Uganda, we were reminded just how important regulatory, institutional and cultural factors are for the creation of innovative and diverse content that is relevant to children, and with which they really want to engage with. We were also reminded about just how good UK provision for children is, even compared with countries that are economically well developed.

Based on the evidence of several workshop participants, it was clear that there was no regulation or virtually no positive regulatory interventions to support children's content in many countries. In the absence of government policy or support measures, combined with the lack of distribution outlets for local content, production communities were not in a position to build the development capacity necessary for supporting local content on whatever platform. Nevertheless local content was clearly seen as a means of forging identities and our participants clearly recognised and understood why public service values mattered when serving children.

In our discussions, universality was acknowledged not just in terms of delivery on widely accessible free platforms, but also in terms of content that was relevant and readily understood by children. Diversity

was understood as opinions, different genres and approaches that had to encompass entertainment if it was going to appeal to children at all. Independence was discussed in terms of independence from the state, but also from corporate and commercial interests linked to advertising and licensed merchandise, and was pivotal in terms of trust. Distinctiveness was seen as closely related to independence and diversity, but in terms of quality is always difficult to define. Some suggested that the only way to assess and measure 'quality' in local children's content was to measure it against both its educational or entertaining purposes, alongside its attractiveness to children, a task that may become harder in a multiplatform universe where content is harder to locate. In these discussions it was the orientation and objectives of public service that mattered to participants, regardless of the platform.

The institution of public service broadcasting might not work for all situations, but the principles underpinning a public service ethos are still valid for a variety of platforms and content, not least because at their very best they prioritise children as young citizens with their own sense of identity, place

and community. The abiding 'takeaway' from this session was that the combination of positive regulatory interventions and funding can provide the framework for diverse, distinctive productions within a supportive ecology of relevant stakeholders. In the closing words of one participant, "The key issues facing people involved in children's screen content are: getting sufficient powers to do what is needed and sufficient funding to make original content that children want to view".

What the BBC has established with BBC Children's is a unique and important marker of its commitment to children in the UK. In a more complicated media landscape, it would help if it spelled out its approach more clearly to the public in the run up to charter review.

This piece is an extended version of an opinion piece that first appeared in the Spring 2015 Bulletin of the Voice of the Listener and Viewer (VLV). The VLV champions excellence and diversity in broadcasting. The author, Jeanette Steemers, is a member of the VLV Board of Trustees (as is the yearbook editor, Lynn Whitaker).

The University of Westminster will be hosting an evening event on 'BBC Children's and Charter Renewal' in association with the Children's Media Foundation and the Voice of the Listener and Viewer on 3 September 2015. Location: University of Westminster

PUBLIC BROADCASTING IN CANADA: KIDS' CBC AND TVOKIDS

KERRIE-ANN BERNARD AND NATALIE COULTER

We both grew up loving the children's shows on our public broadcasters. One of us was a child of the 1970s and grew up watching *The Polka Dot Door, Matt and Jenny,* and *Mr. Dressup* and one of us was a child of the 1990s who loved *Fred Penner's Place, Today's Special* and *Under the Umbrella Tree.* As avid viewers of Canadian children's TV, we never knew that what we were watching was public broadcasting we just knew we loved it enough to spend hours watching it.

Canada has always had a mix of both commercial and public broadcasters who have a long history of producing engaging and popular programming for children. Many shows, such as the *Degrassi* franchise, *You Can't Do That on Television*, and Sharon Lois and Bram's *The Elephant Show*, have enjoyed global success. Public broadcasting in Canada is an interesting blend of French and English services delivered by both a national public broadcaster and provincial broadcasters - all of which produce programming with a public service mandate. On the national level, the Canadian Broadcasting Corporation (CBC) and its French arm Radio-Canada are mandated to produce programming that informs, enlightens, and entertains men, women, and children. While on the provincial level, there are currently four provincially funded public broadcasters. In Ontario there is TVO and

Télévision Française de l'Ontario (TFO), in Québec there is Télé-Québec, and in British Columbia there is Knowledge Network. Alberta and Saskatchewan have also had public provincial broadcasters; however both have since been privatised. These provincial broadcasters are mandated to specifically provide educational programming for persons of all age. In Canada, children's media is broadcast by all of these entities; by commercial broadcasters; by French and English broadcasters; and by national and provincial public broadcasters.

Obviously public broadcasting in Canada is a complicated mesh of many entities. To more closely examine the state of public broadcasting for children in Canada, we will focus specifically on English broadcasters, the CBC and TVO, both of which have dedicated program blocks that focus on children's programming: Kids' CBC and TVOKids.

Children's programming airing on CBC is concentrated during the morning with their Kids' CBC programme block. The mandate of the CBC as a whole is to produce programming that speaks to the experiences of Canadians and the Canadian way of life. In addition to the CBC's overall mandate, it has also developed parameters for their children's programming. In this case the CBC looks to produce programming that fits into their 'whole child strategy'. As such, programming seeks to address social, cognitive, emotional, creative, and physical development in an age-appropriate way. While not necessarily overtly educational, each Kids' CBC program does address some, if not all, of these elements of children's development.

TVO's children's programming (which airs both in the morning as well as after-school), on the other hand, is mandated to meet standards set out by the Ontario school curriculum, so while the CBC's programming is educational and age-appropriate it is not similarly tied to school curricula. As an educational broadcaster, TVO's mandate is to be part of the public education system in Ontario. As such, all children's content must meet the provincial curriculum and TVO works with teachers and educational advisors to create content. As an active part of Ontario's education system, TVO adds further support to the curriculum by providing other aids, such as an online maths site for elementary school children; online homework help with qualified teachers; and a private platform for teachers only to share their lesson plans and discuss teaching issues.

Despite the efforts of both the CBC and TVO, the last decade has left both facing similar obstacles, as the federal and provincial governments that largely fund the broadcasters are repeatedly cutting funds in the name of balancing budgets. At the moment the Conservative Government is slashing CBC's funding, so it is becoming increasingly apparent that our Prime Minister has little respect for the CBC and many surmise that his goal is essentially to shut down the public broadcaster all together. But, while some of the deepest cuts to the CBC have come most recently under Canada's current Conservative government - which appears to have a vendetta against the CBC - this is only a continuation of a trend that started in the 1990s. Since then there has been a deepening of the funding cuts and restructuring to make CBC - and, to a lesser extent, TVO - more market-orientated, shifting their focus away from public service. While both broadcasters still strive to make strong, child-centred educational programming, they are increasingly being hobbled by decreasing budgets.

In addition to funding cuts there are government directives that push the public broadcasters to rely more on private production houses. This has led both CBC and TVO to largely abandon the production of their own inhouse content.

Instead, public broadcasters buy or commission most of their content from both Canadian and international production houses. As a result, the great public broadcasting shows that we both grew up loving, the shows that referenced Canada and had a Canadian sensibility, are, for the most part, no longer being made. Instead much of the original content being produced by TVOKids and Kids' CBC is the interstitial content that runs between the bought shows. Short programmes like TVO's *Gisèle's Big Backyard* and CBC's *Kids' Canada*.

This original interstitial content as well as the few shows that are still made inhouse by CBC such as *Chirp* and *The Adventures of Napkin Man*, are geared to a preschool audience. TVO commissions a significant portion of its content including notable shows such as *Annedroids*, *Odd Squad*, *Doozers* and *Finding Stuff Out*.

Indeed, the majority of programming offered by Kids' CBC and TVO is focused on preschool aged children. This leaves older children (especially aged seven and up) with very little programming geared to them. Youth are virtually ignored by the public broadcasters so they turn to the commercial stations.

Despite all their efforts, both broadcasters are also under increasing pressure to find alternate sources of revenue to show self-sufficiency. This situation necessitates that CBC and TVO compete with commercial broadcasters who have significant budgets, no educative or cultural mandates, and who often emphasise merchandising and licensed goods over content.

The reality of funding cuts and the constant threat of further cuts means that CBC and TVO are increasingly required to justify their legitimacy both to the governments that fund them and to the public at large. It is, during these times of austerity, becoming increasingly difficult to communicate the value of publicly funded children's content to both of these groups. Children's media faces a further battle in that it often even has to struggle to show its value to the station's upper management. However TVOKids and Kids' CBC have found innovative ways of justifying their budgets and indeed their value to their respective institutions.

For TVO the online aids that the station provides to teachers and students deliver valuable metrics. These metrics can be used to illustrate that TVOKids is an integral component of the education system. It is difficult to justify funding cuts if teachers and parents are using the site to enhance their children's education. On the other hand, Kids' CBC, can show their value by pointing to the number of downloads of their apps, the number of visits to their websites and the number of attendees at their live concerts. Additionally, by serving mainly preschool children, Kids' CBC fills a gap in the market and by doing so prove itself to be indispensable in the process. It is important to note that much of this justification is aimed at both upper management and government. Indeed, children's media still has to struggle to show its value to the wider public who, unless they have children, are often oblivious to its existence.

In Canada, particularly in English-speaking Canada, we have little appreciation for the vast repertoire of children's media that has been made. Canadian's speak nostalgically about the Canadian shows they watched as children, but they are often not aware that these shows were made by the public broadcaster, or even that they are Canadian at all. There is here a missed opportunity to remind Canadians of the value of their public broadcasters; to remind them of the rich and diverse content that CBC and TVO have produced for the children's mediascape. As such, TVO and CBC are missing a chance to tap into the good will and nostalgia that their catalogues of immensely popular children's programming could afford them.

With Saskatchewan's provincial public broadcaster being privatised as recently as 2010, the threat to public broadcasting is real in Canada. If we don't rally behind our public broadcasters, they and the children's programming that they do make will be eroded until there is nothing left. What is at stake here for Canadians is not simply educational children's programming produced without a commercial imperative, it is our national identity. ☺

CHILDREN'S PROGRAMMES IN PUBLIC TELEVISION IN POLAND

AGNIESZKA WEGLINSKA

Modern media undoubtedly shapes our world and its place in a young person's life poses a challenge for education. The mission assumption of public media is creating and broadcasting programmes for children. This short review of Polish broadcaster TVP's offer is focused on the youngest viewers and I will begin with a cult programme, *Wieczorynka*. It is on purpose that I begin my description of TVP's offer for children with *Wieczorynka* as the decision to stop broadcasting it caused a turbulent discussion in society and it resulted in the creation of a dedicated children's channel 'TVP ABC'.

Wieczorynka in TVP

Wieczorynka was shown every day at 7pm from 1962 and was very popular. Polish public media inherited the show from television during PRL (Polish People's Republic) times. Before the collapse of communism in Poland, valuable productions dedicated to children were made. Since 1992, the Principal Editorial Television Team for Children Programmes has dealt with creating content for children. The first broadcasted *Wieczorynka* was a programme called 'Jacek i Agatka' (1962) in the form of two puppets whose adventures were supposed to not only entertain but also teach. The animation studios in Łódź, Warsaw and Bielsko Biała created these programmes.

Little local content for children is currently being made for modern Polish television. During children's scheduling slots foreign production were also shown, such as *Bob the Builder* or *The Smurfs*. Between 2010 and 2014 a turbulent debate took place regarding the role and the place of evening TV programmes for children on public television and it was caused by the fact that *Wieczorynka* was losing viewers to dedicated channels and had become too expensive to broadcast for TVP. The president of TVP, Juliusz Brown, noted that "Bedtime shows have a smaller audience, mainly consisting of older people. Children make only 10% and pensioners 30%". There appeared the concepts of creating a public dedicated channel for children and as a result the removal and loss of *Wieczorynka*.

The problem was that, for parents, *Wieczorynka* was still a cult programme: they grew

up with it and felt connected. Those in favour of removing this programme insisted that it was necessary to modernise media education at TVP; give up on didactics; and pursue innovative forms. They showed that a dedicated channel directed at children would be an answer to the rich offer of commercial channels. Those opposing removal of *Wieczorynka* countered that it was an iconic tradition and that children from the poorest environment, or from regions with weak television signal, would suffer most from it being axed.

TVP ABC

Within TVP there is a thematic channel for children aged between 4 and 12 years old. It mainly broadcasts archival TVP productions and foreign content, such as *Chuggington*. At its beginning in February 2014, the channel was announced as television for children totally without violence, and promoting family and national values. The president of TVP, Juliusz Braun said: "content will not include exaggeration and violence. It must be a channel with programmes that 'will always be safe'. This is what parents expect

from broadcasters. Due to the lack of stable financing of public media, there will not be many premieres".

The programmes on offer from TVP ABC include a wide range of programmes for the youngest viewers. It broadcasts a leading programme for children created by the Catholic programming team, *Ziarno* ('The Seed'). In the relevant law on radio and television there is a provision that "Public television does not forget its youngest viewers and therefore it prepares attractive, educational and adventurous programmes for them". Therefore, TVP creates popular science programmes such as *Mission in Space*, described by the TVP editorial team thus: "The programme concerns outer space, interesting phenomena such as black holes, remote galaxies, etc.". Some of the episodes were made in the Copernicus Science Centre (CSC) in Warsaw, the most modern and biggest science museum in Poland. Children from other parts of Poland can take part in the activities organises by CSC by means of television.

An element of language education by means of television can be seen in the programme *Lippy and Messy* which was made by the Children's Television of Programme 1 of TVP along with an English language school Gama-Bell. The show offers interactive games in English for the youngest children. Also worth mentioning is *Supełkowe AB*, a show which albeit addressed to *all* children is especially focused on deaf and or hearing-impaired children. The programme teaches the alphabet, numbers, and phrases necessary to communicate with friends who live in the world of silence. Another proposition, *Culture Behind the Scenes*, is a programme made with the resources and cooperation of National Culture Centre. The narrator of all episodes is thirteen year old Magda who visits interesting places connected with culture.

In the evenings after 10pm, TVP ABC broadcasts lifestyle programmes for parents. There are cooking, interior designer, nature and other programmes. Programmes of this new channel are also available online, its website is interactive, and it is possible to watch archival programmes there and also play games.

Internet Theatre for Schools

Units of public radio and television are obliged to create and popularise programmes for schools and other educational institutions. Traditional television played this role in the case of artistic and cultural education. At the very beginning of Polish television in 1958, a puppeteer Jan Wilkanowski created a series, *Baj, Baj*, which combined fun with introducing a child to the world of art. In the eighties, Sunday afternoon *Television Theatre for Children* was very popular. The shows were made in cooperation with 26 theatres from all over Poland, the data from 1988 indicates that the shows were watched by some 16% of viewers over sixteen, mainly parents with children, which proves the popularity of this undertaking.

Nowadays we might mainly talk about public service media rather than public service broadcasting. In the first two decades of this century we can observe an increase in the significance of internet media. However, there is still internet media which is strongly correlated with social networks and civic broadcasters on the net which take over those tasks assigned to public service media. Media academic Jay Blumler holds this viewpoint, and believes that, through the activities of public service media, the civic sphere benefits because television has taken over the role of animating public debate. The internet media can be used to attract public opinion, but on the other hand they have more autonomy than traditional media.

It is worth pointing out that TVP regional producers are aware of the importance of such internet activities. It is worth quoting Paulina Sitko - an editor from Wroclaw TVP centre: "I consider internet theatre for schools as part of our [public service] mission: e.g. today there was a performance in the Puppet Theatre which was broadcasted via our broadcast vans to 46 schools in Poland, meaning that 18,000 pupils were simultaneously watching it - the

biggest audience in the world."

This is a very important example showing that in favourable conditions public service related media activities are moving to the internet. Of course, it is partly a result of the lower costs for such undertakings. We have to state, though, that in the area of commercial media nobody would commission these broadcasts, as it's a very niche undertaking. So let's not underestimate the fact that children from smaller towns and villages have contact with theatre by means of the net. This is a combined benefit of regional centres, and also of the fact that puppet theatres from all over Poland can perform on a national stage. Programmes for children and teenagers institute an important element of a public service broadcaster's mission; involvement in such projects constitutes a statutory duty of a broadcaster.

It is also important that schools in Poland, even in villages, where internet access can be questionable, have access to the net. Internet theatre for schools relates to similar technological initiatives, which took place in the past, even in PRL times.

Summing up, public media in Poland in the area of content addressed to children shows a tendency to create segments and fragment the market. The channel ABC addresses viewers between four and twelve years old, and it seems appropriate that, in accordance with media market tendencies, TVP should start a channel for teenagers and children under three years old. Removing *Wieczorynka* indicated the end of an era in TVP and the end of a ritual connected with television. The programme stopped playing a part of our childhood and was replaced by a thematic channel that will undoubtedly continue to evolve. ⊙

AOTEAROA/NEW ZEALAND: A SMALL HOUSE WITH BIG WINDOWS

RUTH ZANKER

It is a confusing time for everyone advocating for public service media delivery for children, and it is no different for us in New Zealand. As a researcher and trustee of the New Zealand Children's Screen Trust (kidsonscreen.co.nz) I am struggling to keep up with the explosion of globally accessible platforms and apps targeted at children. These inevitably undermine the viewership for content funded through dedicated national public funding streams. In New Zealand we talk increasingly about how endangered children's local public media spaces have become.

New Zealand research released in April 2015 illustrates that YouTube is now equally popular (for children who have access to internet) as the traditionally dominant Channel Two state-owned broadcaster's scheduled provision. An even more concerning fact for national providers is the news that YouTube is now the *main content discovery site* for older children in New Zealand.

Of course the chaotic consumption of YouTube channels and memes cannot be meaningfully compared with the carefully programmed schedules of national channels (augmented as they are by websites with their curated repeats, interactivity and apps), but the writing seems to be on the wall. As I write YouTube are branding 'safe' global children's channels, albeit with recent glitches serving up scatological and sexual content.

But the new audience research truism is that kids know what they like and will search it out relentlessly. New Zealand children are enthusiastically tapping into reruns of favourite cartoons; the viral news of Pewdiepie; and new apps.

The great question facing a small nation like New Zealand is: How can we enable our children to stumble upon local content in formats they enjoy and on the media platforms they prefer? And where does this leave public service provision for children in New Zealand?

NZ is not a poor nation, but it has never been easy to fund for diversity for 911,000 children across the range of age groups. New Zealand shares challenges facing all smaller and/or poorer countries struggling to find the balance between service and cost when it comes to local media delivery for their children.

There is one thing we need to be clear about from the start: New Zealand has never had pure public service provision (think BBC or ABC). Instead, since 1989, a pared back version of public service provision has been mandated, whereby a funding agency called New Zealand On Air is tasked with "reflecting and developing New Zealand's identity and culture". This model, at first glance, offers an enticing minimalist public service funding solution for nations unable, or unwilling, to pay for full public service provision. But the NZ On Air experiment also presents a cautionary tale or two for nations setting out to establish their own versions of public service delivery to children. This article asks: How does it perform in its core function? And does this equate to public service delivery?

To help us explore these questions it is helpful to focus on four critical factors that comprise public service media for children, as summarised by Jeanette Steemers:

- Universality
- Diversity
- Independence
- Distinctiveness or 'quality'

How then do these apply to the New Zealand experience?

Universality – great content delivered on widely accessible platforms that is relevant and easily understood.
Unsurprisingly for a former British colony, New Zealand's early broadcasting roots drew from the Reithian principles to 'inform, educate and entertain'. But New Zealand politicians demanded a trade-off between *competing* Reithian principles which have shaped our television provision, and now digital delivery.

Broadcast engineers in New Zealand faced the daunting and expensive task of delivering television broadcasts to *all citizens* across an Alpine nation with a scattered population. Whilst the governments might support this nation-building Reithian concept of *universal access*, they demanded a trade-off. Advertising income was made part of the funding mix for state-owned television channels from the very start. Indeed, all successive governments have viewed a pure public broadcasting television service along BBC lines as unaffordable. The Broadcasting funding vote now competes with hip operations and new schools.

As a result, imports and cheap but popular local programming solutions (studio based, presenter led, short shelf life field items) have been favoured by risk averse commercial broadcasters.

The first locally made children's preschool broadcast was a re-versioned BBC *Playschool*. Maori Manu knocked on the door and opened the window to clips of local kiwi family life. American PBS *Sesame Street* became a local staple, this time with Maori language inserts. Maori language television still do extensive dubbing of cartoons into Maori.

The first *locally* created early childhood programme, *You and Me*, only arrived in 1991, after the radical media deregulation of 1989. Deregulation paradoxically embedded an audacious new funding mechanism for local content whilst, at the same time, encouraging commercial competition between state-owned and overseas-owned media.

At this point I would like to extend, for the sake of argument, the notion of *universal access* a bit further. It is a perspective best understood by small/ poor nations. On the face of it, 'quality' global brands like CBeebies, CBBC, The Children's Television Workshop (and Nickelodeon and Disney at their child-centred best) already provide excellent content for children 'universally' (i.e. globally) and across a range of accessible platforms. Take, for example, preschool provision. Don't little children need the same things the world over? Haven't *Teletubbies*, *Blues Clues* and *Sesame Street* delighted very young children everywhere on a range of screens? Local television programmers like them too: translation is cheap and local inserts into indigenous languages are a breeze.

Certainly British public service children's television content has positioned itself for some time in caregivers' minds as a 'quality' brand in New Zealand. Is it, by default, a reliable form of 'public service television' for many New Zealand families (either as programmes filling out local free to air schedules, or on UK pay-channels)? These imported programmes are cheaper than local productions, come with ready-made promotions and with ratings promise.

So we have to ask: Have 'quality global brands' become, by default, *a universal, globally accessible, form of public service* for preschool children at least? If not why not?

The answer is that, so far, New Zealand On Air has consistently funded at least one early years strand on free to air television accessible to all New Zealand preschoolers because it has a mandate to "reflect and develop New Zealand identity and culture" for all New Zealanders, even the tiniest. Our state-owned Channel Two and the overseas-owned Channel Four compete for (low-cost per hour) funding. Early years is the only genre with no ads, thus protecting it from the full force of the market place, although market purists could still view it as 'opportunity cost'.

Diversity: of genres and opinions

It is widely agreed that exposure to a rich diversity of genres and cultural opinion becomes critical for primary-aged children, tweens and youth audiences. Young people mine the media for ideas about being grown up. What is possible? What is not? Who is valued? Who is not?

This is where 'the local' begins to have resonance for small nations like New Zealand who are swamped by media versions of the world forged in American and British focus groups, each with their own particular cultural tensions.

Are children in New Zealand well served with local content inflected by the complex mix of who we are, and where we are positioned in the world? Does our children's media reflect our diverse Pacific set of identities, languages and culture?

The New Zealand On Air mechanism has certainly made a difference. Recent research indicates that both children and parents want local content. Just under 800 hours, costing around $15 million NZ dollars, were funded last round. Award-winning concepts like the unstodgy youth drama *Being Eve* and the science show, *Let's Get Inventin'*, have been grown through its funding. But neither show had a long life. *Being Eve* was scheduled to death by commercial programmers. *Let's get Inventin'* launched an app the very year the broadcaster decided not pitch for further production. It is a constant juggle for producers and New Zealand On Air to get good ideas into production because there is no quota nor licence requirements, nor are there mechanisms to hothouse new concepts in the small marketplace (this of course leads to export success as well). This function of hothousing creative ideas is one of the glories of well-established public service media.

Animation, *the* favourite genre according to children in the recent survey, is deemed too expensive and drama is out of favour with commissioners. But it is this provision of "diversity of genres and range of opinion in local and indigenous stories" that remains central to remnant public service provision for children in New Zealand through New Zealand On Air funding.

Growing and maintaining diversity of provision for children is our biggest challenge. It is very frustrating for producers to have to court broadcasters who have only short term ratings success in mind.

Independence from corporate and commercial interests and the state

So far I have described the implications for children's provision from the trade-off made by successive governments to deliver children's public media on commercial channels. New Zealand On Air is reliant on proposals put forward by commercial channels (the state broadcaster is also commercial remember). These channels are required to have a ratings focus, yet, under current arrangements, have no incentive to promote their children's content (which lives outside prime time).

It is a fragile system because local broadcaster support for desired range and diversity of local content for children is not guaranteed. Furthermore New Zealand On Air is tasked under its 1989 Act to fund only programmes made accessible on free to air channels (and online thereafter). It does not fund behind the pay wall. Nor can it launch new platforms independent of these incumbent commercial broadcasters. Plans to invent full public media for children are very much pipe dreams at the moment.

Quality or 'Distinctiveness'

Despite the challenges outlined above, NZ-based producers, aided by sympathetic commissioners and matchmaking from New Zealand On Air, have traded, juggled and explored new ways of serving local children. Children's producers are nimble and responsive. They research their audiences and care about them. Their teams are often at the cutting edge of new production tools. It is testament to their commitment to the children's area that New Zealand on Air funded children's shows consistently win international awards, despite lack of preproduction development time.

New Zealand On Air is currently developing a funding strategy for diverse multiplatform content that can be found on the platforms children prefer to use. This will launch in mid-2016 and is likely to focus on curation; reviewing functions for parents and navigation tools. The challenge for those designing delivery is that currently there is no new money, nor any political inclination to move the mandate of New Zealand On Air away from first release on the commercially-driven free to air broadcast medium. Watch this space. ◑

JAPAN'S PUBLIC SERVICE BROADCASTING FOR CHILDREN

SACHIKO KODAIRA

What comes to mind when you hear 'children's TV in Japan'? Animation programmes broadcast all day long? Well, it is true that well-known Japanese children's TV programmes such as *Doraemon* and *Pokémon* are both animated cartoons broadcast by commercial TV channels; however, there are many other kinds of TV programming and related online content for Japanese children, which have been developed for various educational purposes by the NHK, our nationwide public broadcaster.

Japan's broadcasting has developed through the coexistence of public broadcaster, NHK (Japan Broadcasting Corporation) - which is supported by the Viewers' Receiving Fee System financially, so is without any advertising - and commercial broadcasters whose source of revenue is income from advertising. Children's programmes started on the very first day of radio broadcasting in 1925, and same also of TV broadcasting in 1953. In this article, I would like to introduce characteristics of children's TV in Japan, focusing on the role of public service broadcasting.

Firstly we should note that children were always regarded as important audiences both by NHK and commercial television, and so a variety of programmes have been developed since the early days of television. After the huge success of the very first TV animation series in Japan, *Astro Boy*, in 1963, a tremendous volume of children's programmes - predominantly a variety of animated cartoons and superhero action dramas - were broadcast on the commercial channels, especially during the 1970s and 1980s. However, they began to decline thereafter because of the difficulty of finding sponsors to support the programmes.

As a public broadcaster, NHK has been providing various genres of programmes since the 1950s: children's drama; puppet shows; games & quizzes; children's news; science shows; as well as studio-based variety shows and entertainment formats that involve children's participation. Also, from the 1970s, animation programmes have been provided. In the early 1990s NHK began to increase its airtime for children, with a schedule including specific programmes for specific age groups. In addition, NHK began to move its children's

programmes - which used to be broadcast on NHK General TV Channel - to NHK Educational TV Channel, established in 1959 as the second NHK channel, for broadcasting programmes for educational purposes (including schools broadcasting.) Most of NHK's programmes for children are shown on this ETV Channel today.

Secondly, TV programmes aimed at preschool children have been produced and broadcast since the early days of television in Japan. The longest running from NHK, *With Mother*, which continues to broadcast today, began in 1959. Moreover, three years prior to that, in 1956, NHK started the two preschool series intended for viewing at daycare centers and kindergartens as a part of NHK School Broadcasting. Though commercial TV had broadcast preschool programmes as well, it could not continue. NHK has been continuously developing new types of programmes for this age group: some such recent examples, all highly evaluated internationally, are *PythagoraSwitch* to encourage problem-solving skills, *Design Ah!* to inspire creative thinking through understanding various designs around us and *Mimicries* to inspire scientific thinking in preschool children.

Thirdly, the majority of children's programmes (and TV programmes as a whole) broadcast in Japan have been produced domestically, though there have been examples of acquisition programmes from other countries: *Sesame Street*; *Thomas the Tank Engine and Friends*; *Shaun the Sheep*; *Curious George* etc. And there are also some dedicated channels for children, such as Japanese Kids Station and ANIMAX, and US Disney channel and Cartoon Network in satellite channel services, but the penetration rates of these pay channels with additional fees is very limited in Japan, partially because we have been broadcasting quite a number of children's programmes on terrestrial channels both in NHK and commercial TV for a long time.

Fourthly, the existence of two types of programming for children (or two viewing styles) is another feature of Japanese (NHK's) children's TV: programmes for viewing at home with family; and programmes for viewing with friends at schools and kindergartens/daycares with educational guidance by teachers. The latter is called School Broadcasting. Radio school broadcasting started in 1935, ten years after the start of radio broadcasting and TV school broadcasting in 1953, at the same time as the commencement of TV broadcasting in Japan.

Although nowadays children's programmes usually have websites which provide child viewers with various interactive activities related to the broadcast content, NHK's School Broadcasting has taken a leading role to utilise the digital technology effectively for children since the 1990s, an important mission of a public broadcaster.

After seeking and developing new forms of educational services, in 2001 NHK released an online service called *NHK Digital Curriculum* providing free of charge video and interactive-learning and teaching materials that tie in with the content of school broadcast programmes. The use of this new digital service has been increasing gradually among Japanese schools over the past fifteen years, and the use of NHK's educational services for schools in the classroom is beginning to diversify, with schools using the broadcast and digital services sometimes in conjunction and sometimes separately.

Today over 2,000 full-length programme episodes (10-15 minutes each) from over 70 broadcast programme titles and 5,000 short video clips are available on demand on the *NHK for School* website. This site also offers fun learning games and materials to use on interactive whiteboards. With search engine, curated content and recommendations, children have all the tools and guidance they need to explore any subject on their own.

NHK School Broadcasting deals with a wide variety of subjects such as Japanese language, maths, science, social studies, and moral education. Each programme engages the target age groups with songs, dancing, drama, skits, puppet theatre and more. Helping children to think for themselves is an important goal of NHK's school services. There are various programmes to inspire children's curiosity and promote self-expression. *Think Like a Crow!* inspires children to learn how to think scientifically and *The Power of Logic* encourages logical thinking through a school-based drama setting. To inspire children to take action and become a driving force for change is another important goal of NHK's school services. *Knock Out Bullying!* is a series to nurture group awareness that leads to decisive action against any form of bullying, based on the actual experiences of elementary and junior high school students across Japan. *Learning Disaster Prevention* examines what happens in different forms of natural disaster and encourages children to think themselves about how to be prepared for an emergency. Programmes for media literacy education, such as *The Media Eyes* and *Smartphone Real Story*, are produced also for this goal and prepare young people for the real-world challenges they will face.

As already introduced, Japanese children watch mostly locally-made TV programmes; however, this does not mean that we are NOT interested in other societies and cultures. NHK has been involved in different kinds of international co-productions in children's and educational programmes. Moreover, NHK has contributed to the development of educational media around the world, through an important international event.

Discover Science is an edutainment science series, whose main target audience is children aged ten to twelve. It started as a co-production by NHK, NHK Educational Corporation and the Al Jazeera Children's Channel (JCC Qatar in 2010. Later on, broadcasters in Germany, Sweden and Taiwan have joined as co-production partners, and this series has been picked up by broadcasters across the world. In Japan, NHK has been broadcasting this series as a 15-minute programme both for school use and for family viewing.

NHK has been involved in international programme-exchange projects for children's better understanding of other people and other societies and cultures, especially children's lives in other regions. In the ABU Children's Drama co-production series, participants each produce a 15-minute drama episode starring children between seven and nine who are trying to achieve something, and dramas are exchanged among participants and broadcast on each of their channels under a networked principle of 'make one episode and take all others'. For the tenth anniversary of this project in 2014, the ten programmes were broadcast in Japan during summer vacation on NHK Educational TV Channel, and are now available on the NHK for School website.

EBU Youth Documentary Exchange is another co-production project in which, since 2009, NHK has been participating. The mandate is to create a 15-minute documentary targeted at ten to twelve year olds, and the participants are able to bring back for broadcasting the programmes made by others. NHK produces additional stories other than the programme submitted for the EBU exchange project and broadcasts that content as a School Broadcast series (along with web resources) entitled *Colourful: Children of the World*. So far more than 140 children from over 20 countries have been introduced within this series.

NHK has contributed to the development of educational media around the world for 50 years as an organizer of the international contest called the 'Japan Prize'. This contest was established by the NHK in 1965 to enhance the quality of educational broadcasting around the world and promote international understanding. Today, its target expands to all forms of audio-visual educational media, including TV, websites, games and cross-media projects.

The Japan Prize is not only about selecting winners. It has provided important opportunities for the participants (producers, researchers, and educators) - drawn from all over the world - to engage in open-minded discussion about the entered works in the contest; to exchange views and information; and to develop ideas for future educational media. The Japan Prize is dealing with educational media for all generations; however, "For our children's future" has been its important motto from the very beginning. Fruitful discussions about the potential of education and the future of our children around the world will be expected in this coming Japan Prize 2015 which will be taking place in October as its 50th anniversary.

It is hoped then that this article can set the context not only for Japanese public service media for children but for how other international producers and researchers may wish to engage with it and understand it in the shared interests of the children's audience at large.

ON PRIVATE PUBLIC-SERVICE BROADCASTING FOR KIDS

RUSSELL MILLER

WONDERREEL

Once upon a time, US broadcasting offered two choices to kids: TV... or Educational TV.

Educational TV was the USA's first attempt at public service broadcasting. It was paid for by foundations and the government, not ad revenue. It ran newsy features at night, university lectures in the morning and during the school day, programmes meant to spice up classroom life. After school, I remember a lady reading— literally just sitting there and reading - *David Copperfield*.

During school vacations, there were Chaplin shorts.

TV was everything else.

TV was what Cy Schneider, the [m]ad man who invented the Barbie commercial, meant when he wrote "television's first mission is not to inform, educate or enlighten. It isn't even to entertain. Its first mission is to entice viewers to watch the commercials." Schneider made no exception for children; the quotation comes from his handbook, *Children's Television: The Art, The Business, and How It Works*.

TV could nonetheless strive

for quality. Even as a boy, I'd heard of legendary series like *Kukla, Fran and Ollie*, *Winky Dink and You* (which Bill Gates reputedly called "an early example of interactive TV") and the original *Mickey Mouse Club*. True, all three had been cancelled by the time I was old enough to watch, and it was inconceivable that I might ever be able to see any of them in those days before VCRs, DVDs, Blu-ray or on-demand networked streaming digital video. But I'd heard of them.

True, as well, all three of

those series were cancelled on Cy Schneider's terms. Take *The Mickey Mouse Club*: if Wikipedia is to be believed, that classic failed because "the Disney studios did not realize high-profit margins from merchandise sales, the sponsors were uninterested in educational programming for children, and many commercials were needed in order to pay for the show." Other sources mention a ratings decline. Weak licensing, poor ad sales, low ratings and the smell of education: and today these are still the Four Horsemen riding roughshod over quality children's TV.

So much for TV. As far as Educational TV goes, it's called 'public' nowadays, and it entertains grown-ups with costume dramas from ITV, BBC comedy and documentaries on neuroscience and a cappella doo-wop. Yet when it comes to children, public television in the US is, well, it's educational. More educational than ever.

Don't get me wrong: PBS Kids is generally genuinely brilliant. *Mister Rogers' Neighborhood* and *Sesame Street* have helped generations of preschoolers learn to count, alphabetise and manage their feelings. Older kids have been encouraged to read by *The Electric Company* and *Super*

Why!, while shows like *Curious George* and *Cyberchase* lay foundations for science and math. (Full disclosure: I've consulted on PBS media past and future.)

These are charming, meticulously crafted shows, and they even move merchandise. But, goodness gracious, they're more set on kids learning than even that worthy lady with *David Copperfield*.

They need to be. It's effectively the law in the US, because since 1993 children's series produced for public service broadcasters have depended on the Federal 'Ready to Learn' Act. That is, the United States Congress is footing the bill, through the United States Department of Education. Ready to Learn grants have, historically, required math, science or reading objectives. Today they expect funded shows to align with formal school standards.

All of which brings me back to Cy Schneider, Kukla, Fran, Ollie, Winky Dink, Mickey Mouse, Chaplin and, yes, that lady reading Dickens. I respect commercial television's need for ad revenue, and I honor PBS Kids' lofty, legislated goals. But children have legitimate interests and needs beyond reading, math or even learning what to do with the mad that you feel. They

deserve opportunities to play and explore and ponder new worlds and ideas and culture and history and art. They deserve entertainment choices richer than the Scylla of enticement to watch commercials and the Charybdis of government-mandated academic learning.

But how?

That involves three questions:

- Where might such entertainment choices come from?
- How might one bring them to kids?
- Who will pay?

Our answers are the bedrock of the project we've embarked on. It's called Wonderreel©.

Where might such entertainment choices come from?

All over the world, it turns out. For instance, year after year, fine children's television - series and one-offs - is screened at two inspiring festivals: in even years, the Prix Jeunesse International in Munich, and, in odd ones, the ComKids Prix Jeunesse Iberoamericano in Sao Paulo. Meanwhile, in Brazil, in the Netherlands, in Germany, in Sweden, Norway and beyond, kids' films produced for cinemas are every bit as accomplished as those made for grown-ups. And the UK is home to a trove in the Children's Film Foundation collection, administered by the Children's Media Foundation and the British Film Institute.

How might one bring them to kids?

Through on-demand networked streaming digital video, on tablets and laptops and phones and connected TVs. Think of Wonderreel© as an HBO Now for kids, available by low-price subscription.

By the way, anytime/anywhere digital affects more than just *delivery* of content. It can fundamentally change children's entertainment. With physics itself constraining timeslots in conventional TV, even public service broadcasters seek out shows with broad popular appeal. By moving television to the cloud, Wonderreel© can offer thousands of choices to millions of kids at any given moment. By employing 'Recommendations' technology, complementarily, we can match each child with shows that s/he is likely to love. This is more than mere curation: a better metaphor is the friendly librarian. Wonderreel© can make television as personal and rewarding as finding the right book.

Who will pay?

Ah, the fun part. First of all: No one who wants to advertise to kids; but not taxpayers either, nor the government. Wonderreel© is a business, funded by investors at first and later by the families we'll serve. But we're a new kind of business (at least in the US). We're a "public benefit corporation," or "B-corp".

However a B-corp is not not-for-profit. It's very much a business intent on reaping profits with solid return to investors. But neither is a B-corp a corporation in the usual sense: because its charter encompasses public service goals.

Like digital delivery, public service charters change everything; they up-end the meaning of "decisions in the company's best interests". Chartered to public service, a B-Corp's management can - indeed must - make decisions which advance its social mission, not only its bottom line. For instance, B-Corps can choose to give their services and goods away to people who can't afford to be paying customers (and many B-corps do, distributing everything from sneakers to sunglasses). B-Corp status provides legal protection for ethical practice. And it's hard to imagine an industry whose customers deserve ethical practice more than ours.

Public service broadcasting in the US has come a long way from recorded university lectures. But whether by constraint, preference or tradition, its outstanding educational service offers but a small slice of the possibilities AV content - and indeed the world itself - holds for kids. Marshalling innovations in technology and law, Wonderreel© proposes a new model of children's entertainment. In the process, we find ourselves pioneering a new form of entertainment provider: the private public-service, *narrow-* (in the sense of individualized), but, collectively, more *broad*-than-our-forerunners-ever imagined-*caster*.

With Beta tests on track for this autumn, soon enough, we'll find out if it works.

INDUSTRY REFLECTIONS AND DEBATES

BRINGING TOYS-TO-LIFE

ANDY ROBERTSON

Small plastic figurines that unlock characters in the video games children play have become almost unavoidable over the four years since Activision launched Skylanders *Spyro's Adventure* on an unsuspecting world.

As a journalist specialising in video games for families this is a trend I've covered in detail. There are both positives and negatives to the trend, but unquestionably it's driven by its ability to modularise both video game development and purchasing options offered to young consumers.

There are now four main titles in this space. Skylanders, Disney Infinity, Amiibo and LEGO Dimensions. Each of these have substantial differences but are united by the way they are sold and the technology that powers them.

Hybrid toy-video games enter the home when a family

purchases a starter pack. This costs in the region of £70-£100 and provides the USB peripheral that plugs into a video game console and 'reads' the related toys that are placed on it. The starter pack will also include the game disc and two or three toy characters to get players started. The packs also include secondary items such as collectable stats cards and items that unlock more minor content.

The video game is played on any of the current crop of consoles; Wii U, Xbox 360, Xbox One, PlayStation 3 and PlayStation 4. Some games, like Skylanders, continue to support older platforms like the Wii and are testing out tablet versions as well.

Toys That Unlock Video-Game Media

This 'Toys-to-Life' genre, a term coined by Activision, are game changers for interactive children's media because of the interplay between physical and virtual characters. While playing the game, placing a toy character on the USB peripheral (a circular pad with space for a few toys called a Portal in Skylanders, Base in Infinity and Toy Pad in LEGO Dimensions) instantly brings them into the video game as a playable character with no wires or buttons to press.

The real action is happening on the screen like any other video game, but the physical toy needs to be present on the peripheral sat beside the console. Any progress or character customisations are instantly saved back to the toy, again with no buttons needing to be pressed. It makes the play experience simple and seamless and creates a strong connection between the toy and on-screen character.

Children can take their toy character to a friend's house and use it in their game (no matter which console they have). Placing their toy on a friend's peripheral instantly brings their customised character into the game.

This offers a great novelty to young players, but also locks away content and levels until you purchase additional characters on top of the starter pack. The games are updated each year along with a new set of 20-30 new characters to collect.

Although you can complete the game with just the starter pack you won't see all the content on the game disc without buying a good number of additional toy characters that cost between £7-15 each new. Purchasing a new toy figure and putting it on the Portal/Base/Toy-Pad enables you to use the related character as well as often unlocking new areas and powers.

These additional characters and levels are usually signposted to players with short optional video adverts showing what you could access if you owned the particular toy. Although parents are used to advertising of this nature in TV programs, this kind of promotion within a video game is less expected and is effective at driving pester power at supermarket and toy store checkouts.

The bottom line is that although it would cost hundreds of pounds to collect all the toys in a particular range, the majority of the game can be played to completion without purchasing additional toy figures. This typically provides a basic twelve-hour adventure with multiplayer and additional missions that are likely to extend playing time to well over 20 hours. Armed with this information, parents need to be willing and able to say no to requests for ever more toy figures.

All Toys (To Life) Are Not Equal

Adding new toys is not always straightforward, not least because of the complexity that has developed year on year with each range. In fact one selling point being pushed by LEGO Dimensions is that you don't need complicated compatibility charts to understand which characters will work with the game. Time will tell whether LEGO is able to maintain its simple universal compatibility in subsequent years any better than competitors.

Skylanders does a reasonable job of supporting all the old toy figures in the new games. This ensures that children who invest in toy Skylanders have an ongoing value in being able to use their old toys in each new game. A rule of thumb is to stick to characters with packaging that matches the game you own.

Children may at times insist they understand which characters will work but even experts struggle to identify some of the nuances of compatibility. This fact is underlined by erroneous compatibility charts in store. Although some may suggest this is a cynical ploy on Activision's part, I think it's more a measure of the complexity.

Disney Infinity adds further complication as it is really two games in one. Not only does it have an adventure element but also an excellent game creator mode. While you can use any of the toy characters you have purchased in the game creator Toy Box mode, only characters matching a particular brand can be used in the Playset adventures.

Furthermore, if you purchased Disney Infinity 1.0 you can download an upgrade to the 2.0 Toy Box but there is no way to upgrade and access the Disney Infinity 2.0 Playset adventure packs. Families have to purchase another Starter Pack if they want to play the Marvel adventures in this year's game, even if they already own a starter pack from the original game.

The same is true the other way round. If you have purchased Disney Infinity 2.0 you can't access the *Toy Story*, *Pirates of the Caribbean*, *Lone Ranger*, *Cars*, *Incredibles* and *Monsters University* adventures without purchasing the 1.0 Starter Pack as well. You can use all the old toy characters in the Toy Box but not access their bespoke adventure Playsets.

Although I don't consider this a purely commercial ploy, families would have the ability to download any Playset adventure for a related toy purchase higher on their priority list than Disney. Happily, Disney Infinity 3.0 promises to resolve much of this by offering a stand-alone disc or download version of the new game.

Additionally, and at risk of losing those who have kept up so far, both Skylanders and Infinity offer a secondary line of products for retail with more

minor functions in the game. Skylanders Trap Team enables players to play as the villains they encounter if they have purchased the appropriate plastic 'trap' to place in the Portal at the right moment. Disney Infinity offers Power Discs that are placed under the toy characters to add upgrades, costumes and special powers. Both these cost just a few pounds each, although the Infinity Power Discs were sold in foil blind packs resulting in doubles - something being switched for labelled Power Discs this year for Disney Infinity 3.0.

Nintendo's Amiibo range of smart video game-toy characters escape much of this confusion by being compatible with a wide range of games and don't require a starter pack. Although the 'amiibos' are sold in relation to one game in particular, as is depicted on their packaging, they are compatible with any Nintendo title that has amiibo functions for that character. Identifying which games a particular amiibo is compatible with is something parents (or children!) will need to research online.

Unlike Skylanders and Disney Infinity, amiibo characters function as a companion or opponent character in the game. Bringing a Mario amiibo into *Super Smash Bros.* on the Wii U for example brings in a Mario who will fight for or against you rather than a character you control yourself. Also, because both the Wii U and New 3DS have the NFC technology built into them already, you don't need to purchase a USB peripheral to use amiibos.

LEGO Dimensions is the latest addition to the Toys to Life genre and looks to correct some of the shortcomings of its competitors. Firstly, being LEGO, the characters are much more in the toy vein. Rather than collectable figurines to be displayed on a shelf, the toys in LEGO Dimensions have much more play value, epitomised by the fact that players have to build the USB peripheral out of LEGO bricks before using it with the game — added value parents will appreciate.

Another nice touch is that the different franchise characters will be completely interoperable. Unlike the Disney Infinity adventures that only support one brand, LEGO Dimensions will enable players to mix and match characters throughout the game — as they would playing with physical toys on the living room floor. Again this adds to the perceived value for parents.

The Outer Limits
Anki Drive is one of a number of products that engage children

in media both physically and virtually. However, whereas the gaming action takes place on the screen for the likes of Skylanders, Infinity and Dimensions, for Anki Drive it's on the living room carpet.

Toy cars race around a large printed circuit. The cars automatically keep themselves on course leaving the child to change lanes, control the speed and fire weapons via a connected Smartphone or Tablet device. This also enables the game to narrate the action and have characters interact with players before, during and after the race via the screen. Computer opponents can be loaded into cars to offer a single player option.

The Anki Drive Starter Pack is £150, a price tag that increases by the requirement of a smartphone or tablet, along with additional cars that retail around £50: but for families who already have the devices it offers an unusual and accessible experience for players of all ages. The new version - Anki Overdrive - also offers a Scalextric style clip together track system and support for mixing iOS and Android controllers.

App games too are also leveraging this physical crossover market. Angry Birds is perhaps

most significant here with its Telepods. These unlock characters in their range of games and are sold as physical play packs with racing and projectile play patterns.

Games like Angry Birds Go! made good use of this, although with a complex retail model. Characters could be purchased either digitally in-app or unlocked with the physical toys; so it is at times hard to determine which is the best value.

Keeping digital purchase prices high may have intended to drive toy sales but instead seems to have resulted in a confused economy of purchases with a slower take-up at retail; add to this the fact that Telepods are optional extras rather than essential to the experience like Skylanders, Infinity and Dimensions toys.

The Future
The Toys-to-Life category continues to grow, albeit not at the rate of the early explosion when Skylanders launched. Having that head start, Activision's Skylanders series is still the biggest in terms of total sales with over 240 million toys sold driving more than $3 billion in lifetime revenue.

Growth has slowed as competitors have joined the sector that is fast becoming saturated. Each of the main three offerings has distinct benefits and costs for young players.

- Skylanders offers endearing original characters crafted by its artisan inhouse designers which escape the usual commercial buff/slender binary for male/female heroes. It also supports every one of its toy figures in every new game, placing no restriction on their use in new adventures.

- Disney Infinity offers not only widely loved characters but also draws from its wide catalogue with Marvel and Star Wars. It also offers a comprehensive game-maker Toy Box mode where children can make and share their own games with educational benefits.

- LEGO Dimensions again draws from a wide range of LEGO, DC Comics and Warner franchises, but also leverages the (much loved) brick building of LEGO toys. Also, this is the only Toys to Life product that really offers a proper toy rather than collectable figurine.

- Amiibo toys work with multiple games on the Wii U, offering children ongoing value in unlocking extra content and features from a single purchase. They also don't need a starter pack as the reader technology is already built into the Wii U controller and New 3DS/3DS XL.

- Anki Overdrive extends physical racing robot cars into the video game space with characters, stories and upgradable virtual weapons. This year's game will offer customisable clip together tracks complete with crossovers, banked corners and jumps.

Currently the drive to offer children a new experience every year is strong, but with the level of investment required to develop the toy and video game media it's likely that this will move to less frequent major releases and more ongoing updates.

The current Toys-to-Life physical products largely are collectable, non-articulated figures. With the advent of LEGO's more playable smart toys we are likely to see the technology hidden inside more traditional toy forms rather than the current trend of housing it in a circular base. This will open more options for physical play in addition to the on-screen action, something that parents will perceive as better value.

There are plenty of commercial cards in play here, as these games have proved it possible to make strong profits from movie tie-in titles for young players - something that has previously been elusive. Equally though, publishers understand the importance for parents to perceive these expensive investments as good value, even if those perceptions are pushed to the limit.

Either way the trend is certainly here to stay in some form or other. While buying a big starter pack every year may soon have had its day, using media to create a close interactive relationship between children and their toys is still a powerful way to connect video games to the real world.

TAMING THE FUTURE – PERSPECTIVES ON THE DIGITAL WORLD FROM BBC CHILDREN'S

DANIEL BAYS AND JON HAYWOOD

The King ('TV') is dead, long live the King ('Digital') – right?

Wrong! Well, at least, it's not quite as simple as that; although 'linear TV viewing' still dominates children's media time, watching content on a TV screen is in steady decline and has been for some time; it has the potential to be overtaken by 'time on the internet' as early as 2016.[1]

However, this is not due to a dominant digital usurper winning some kind of technological tournament. The reality is that content that might once have been called 'TV' or shown as 'linear TV' is now being made available and consumed on any number of other screens alongside entertainment and information sources and, as a result, is also evolving. 'Digital' is the next evolutionary step for media: an enrichment of our experiences of content rather than a replacement. This phenomenon is not just limited to TV, it is happening across the media landscape and throughout all areas of children's lives.

Our audiences, viewers and browsers, are 'Born Digital' – the whole CBeebies audience (children 0-6) doesn't know a world without touch screens, apps, tablets and smartphones; 66% of 7-16 year olds own a smartphone; 45% of 5-16s own a tablet.[1] Children inhabit a world flooded with digital

ESCARGOT ESCAPE ARTISTES

content choices (300 hours of video are uploaded to YouTube every minute[2]). Platforms are increasingly or entirely digital (between 2012 and 2014, BBC iPlayer requests from handheld devices rose from 29% to 59%[3]). Our tools and delivery systems are now mostly digital and more content is being consumed (and generated) digitally than ever before (5-16s spend on average 6.3 hours of media time each day;[1] 73% of 6-12s now use YouTube at least once a week[4]).

Essentially, right now, it seems to be a case of 'digital or doomed'.

So, what can we do to survive and thrive?

First, because everything is already digital or becoming digital, the term is almost becoming meaningless so we'd better define what we mean: for us, 'digital' refers to an approach to content, experiences, platforms and audiences that, at a minimum, utilises and, at best, actively exploits and attempts to optimise

the opportunities afforded by the internet and new technology and modes of interaction.

As for 'what can we do to survive and thrive?', we've all been asking this same question for many years – both in BBC Children's and the wider industry – however, with technology, audience behaviours, platforms and content all changing and augmenting at such a terrific pace (and, in fact, the rate of change itself is accelerating), it's a question that doesn't have a single or reliable answer.

So as we attempt to find the best way forward, we have uncovered a few insights that we'd like to share:

Boundaries are blurring

It used to be that discrete teams made defined content or products for specific platforms. Now that platforms are all interconnected and genres have dissolved and merged, content and products are no longer separate entities but experiences on a single continuum. Teams have a wider view and deliver value across multiple platforms.

For instance, one could now argue that games and TV/video content should no longer be considered as separate genres but, instead, two forms of 'Digital Storytelling' on a single spectrum of increasing interactivity: images (e.g. memes and Instagram imagery) at one end and fun digital toys at the other.

In response to this boundary blurring, BBC Children's has softened and blurred its boundaries to enable mixing, merging and increasing collaboration between the classic: 'TV', 'Online' and 'Platforms' teams and specialisms (in CBeebies we're very lucky and proud to add 'Radio' to that list too and, with *Hetty Feather*

Ghost Stories, CBBC can add 'Audio' also) and attempted to improve collaboration with our many partners in the indie sector. We've found that the best production teams now don't conform to previous rigid definitions and have porous boundaries to allow mixing of specialisms and optimal cooperation with others. Although there's still a lot of work to do, we have some great examples, of which we are really proud, and we are always looking to moving forward and improve:

Let's Go Club, a CBeebies inhouse production, will be a truly multiplatform production in CBeebies, with seamlessly interlinked online and TV presence – a dynamic, active online hub that provides content for a fun weekly TV show that inspires the main online activities in the following week – continuing in a loop. The mixed production team will deliver a range of content and digital experiences every day over the summer holidays.

Appsolute Genius, from CBBC inhouse production in association with Aardman Digital, sees Dick and Dom enthuse their audience to become app makers. A competition allowed the amazing twelve year old Alex from Hampshire to

make his game Escargot Escape Artistes – featuring a Parisian snail escaping from the clutches of an Eiffel Tower chef. The show inspired great interest from and engagement with the audience and the game became the fastest downloaded app in CBBC history.

Enhance engagement by using each platform to its best potential

The devices and platforms that exist today offer a great many ways to experience and engage with content. A key challenge and opportunity is to find ways to use each of these devices to their best possible potential.

To this end, CBBC has experimented with two dual screen shows/experiences: *Ludus* (Cube Interactive / Boom Pictures) and *Horrible Histories: Gory Games* (Citrus TV / Lion TV) are both quiz show formats using audio-watermarking to allow the audience to join in and play along on mobile devices in real time and compare their performance with on-screen contestants.

There are a great many challenges with this approach but it has proved popular and is definitely an area beginning to come in to its own and add value within children's and, in particular, in the family media landscape (e.g. *The Voice, X Factor, Million Pound Drop*).

As we explore opportunities on other platforms, we are starting to develop original content for our YouTube channels too. CBeebies, in particular, has seen growing success on YouTube through launching bespoke brand-related content, like our comical, alternative 'red-carpet' experience at the cinema premiere of *The Furchester Hotel* (CBeebies In-house Productions & Sesame Workshop).

Using different approaches to content on multiple platforms can also help to reach new audiences too:

Fly High and Huggy (Darrall MacQueen), is a multiplatform, multi-screen 'crossover' show: a series of fun, comedy action games and short-form animation on BOTH CBeebies and CBBC aimed specifically at reaching the audience that might otherwise fall between the two.

Different approaches can also help to reach existing and new audiences better too: in 2014, our websites and online products were all made 'responsive' – meaning that each element/ product made works on all of our platforms, optimising production efficiency, reach and user experience.

Empowerment trumps experiences

Give a child a game and they will *play*. Empower a child with tools and knowledge and they'll *play for longer and* keep coming back (whilst also learning)!

Because children are so comfortable and confident with creative activities on touch screen devices from an early age, we really wanted to create a product that would enable them to creating their own apps and games simply and quickly, and learn at the same time.

In response, we created 'Make It: Technobabble' (CBBC inhouse production and Aardman Digital): a game-maker tied to a popular TV brand that engages users with simple computational thinking while allowing them to concentrate on crafting amazing games by dragging, placing and tweaking simple components.

This simple but powerful tool was launched without full functionality to gauge and respond to audience feedback and, even given this, found that engagement sustained for much longer than any previous CBBC game and so reach grew.

Make fast, release early and innovate WITH the audience not AT them

Three times a week, almost every week of the year, teams from BBC Children's visit schools and youth groups to test our brands, characters, stories and digital products and research our audiences – including, recently, transforming a disused shop in a Leeds shopping centre into the 'CBeebies Lab' to test new games and content with passers-by.

With one million unique downloads in the first nine weeks,[5] the CBeebies 'Playtime' app (CBeebies inhouse production in association with Mobile Pie) was launched in August 2013 in response to our audiences love of 'snackable' and mini-games (it continues to be BBC Children's most successful app (4.2 million downloads to date – May 2015[5]).

After identifying 'Stories' as the second favourite content genre for under sixes, CBeebies developed and launched its second app – CBeebies 'Storytime' (CBeebies inhouse production) – to encourage reading and shared, family experiences.

Downloads grew quickly but then flattened out; audience comments and feedback made it clear that they wanted more stories. The inhouse team responded quickly and designed a brand new, intuitive story management system. App-users will be able to download and remove books from the app whenever they want and choose from a much larger range of stories from a broad selection of CBeebies favourites. This innovative update inspired entirely by user feedback will be available this summer.

Don't forget that parents are digital too

The young parents of today have never really known a world without the internet.

CBeebies is the part of the BBC that engages with and provides the vast majority of content specifically for parents regarding parenting issues. This engagement has clearly been a great contributing factor to the continuing extraordinary success of the brand; CBeebies currently has 150k likes on Facebook,[6] we're also active on Twitter and have just launched a new CBeebies page on the aspirational platform, Pinterest.

We have extended our brand presence and developed our content to be more parent focused too, with six, factual BBC iWonder guides written by academics and other child development experts and covering topics from 'fussy eating' to exploring your child's emotional readiness for school.

These extensions of our work

in CBeebies – in particular on social media – have helped us to reach new and typically difficult to reach audiences, connecting in particular with young females from every demographic.

We're going to need a bigger boat...

The demand for innovation and new and/or more connected services and content is greater than ever before however, attempting to meet these demands raises a great many, often contradictory challenges, for example:

- We must not only allow our audiences to connect and share freely but also limit and protect them to ensure they are safe.
- We must provide the broadest, most diverse possible range of content but also facilitate personalisation and connect with children's individual passions, needs and interests.

We've always put audiences at the heart of what we do, but we now want to put them in the driving seat of the BBC experience. First steps were announced earlier this year of how we're going to do this. Internally, we've been calling this 'myBBC'. It is being developed as a response to the above, attempting to take steps toward

addressing some of these needs, challenges and conflicts (see Phil Fearnley's BBC blog for more). We're actively working on how we deliver this for under-eighteens and families in the optimal and safest way.

Online safety continues to be a priority for us and we are always looking for creative ways to engage kids in this important issue. For example, *Dixi* (Kindle Entertainment) is CBBC's first ever online comedy drama and is about a fictitious social network. Through webisodes/ vlogging, companion content, interactive web chats and even a mock social network, children can explore the above issues and more, e.g. the potential dangers of social networking, online privacy, safety settings, and cyber bullying.

And because the demands for 'community' and 'social' connection and interaction are not just limited to older children, CBeebies is also working on ways to engage and prepare younger audiences for these wider, more connected experiences. *Let's Go Club* is, for the first time, offering the CBeebies audience the opportunity to create and then upload their own content to share on the pre-moderated online hub and within the show's video content too.

We are all active participants in making the digital future

As the playground of the BBC's future mainstream audience, BBC Children's has always been a pathfinder department and we continue to be just that: working together with many internal and external and indie partners, blazing a trail into the digital future. And it's so important that we work closely with other BBC teams to decide how best to serve the young people that make up *our* audience today, but are racing *their* way.

We're doing this in the knowledge that the increasing rate of development, technological evolution and digital acceleration make it impossible to predict what's around every digital corner. But does this mean it's impossible to predict what to do for the best? Or that we're actually fighting a losing battle? We're certain it doesn't!

It has been said that the best way to predict the future is to invent it and, right now, it's children – our audiences – who are doing just that. So, perhaps we should stop trying to predict and take control of the digital future and focus instead on what we can do for our audiences now to better engage with and listen to them; and to develop content and tools to inspire, empower and prepare them.

Perhaps if we do this right then, we can let the digital future take care of itself. ⊙

REFERENCES

1 Childwise Monitor: 'Connected Kids 2015' (April 2015)

2 YouTube Stats (May 2015): https://www.youtube.com/yt/press/en-GB/statistics.html

3 BBC iStats AV (May 2015)

4 Ipsos Media CT – BBC Children's Tracker (Base: All 0-12s = 281, All 6-12s = 141).

5 Relevant app stores (May 2015)

6 Facebook (14th May 2015)

A PERSONAL EXPERIENCE OF ANIMATION POLICY IN PRACTICE

KEN ANDERSON

Director Rachel Bevan Baker and I established Red Kite in December 1997 with a five-minute commission, from Claire Kitson at Channel 4, called *Bee Lines*. The company set itself up in the storeroom of the Edinburgh Film Workshop Trust and, after a lick or two of paint, work began in earnest in early 1998.

In 2001 we were introduced to Sheldon Wiseman, of Amberwood Productions in Canada, to work together on a preschool series entitled *The Secret World of Benjamin Bear*, as an official UK-Canada Treaty co-production. What made this possible was a tax relief based financing incentive in the UK at the time called 'Sale and Leaseback'.

There have been varying forms of British film-related tax reliefs intended to support UK producers and stimulate external investment. Fortunately for Red Kite, by 2001 the definition of British Film included animated TV series. As a small independent producer, we knew about Sale and Leaseback but we really didn't know how it worked or how to use it. Through working with Amberwood and talking with the people in the UK who worked to provide the funding – at that time Film Trading Partnerships – we began to understand how this type of financing could help us to fund our shows. Initially it felt like something only available to the big companies: those with lawyers and accountants on hand. It wasn't until early 2002 that the penny dropped and we realised that it might be something we could market to international partners.

By February 2002 we were in the process of completing and submitting paperwork to the Canadian tax authorities for the production of *The Secret World of Benjamin Bear*. We marketed ourselves at MIPTV in Cannes that April using Sale and Leaseback to unlock new opportunities. The market went very well and I was in high spirits as I took the bus to Nice airport.

While I was sitting in the departure lounge, I received a phone call to inform me that the then Chancellor, Gordon Brown, had, *that morning,* announced the removal of television – including animation series – from the Sale and Leaseback qualifying status. Section 99 of the Finance Act 2002 restricted the relief to films "genuinely intended for theatrical release": this was in large part due to concerns regarding tax avoidance and, most significantly, abuses by the producers of soap operas. So just when we, the little guys on the margins of TV land, had understood how Sale and Leaseback worked, it was snatched away from us due to the opportunistic greed of those that needed it least.

But all was not lost: due to Amberwood already having filed their application to the authorities in Canada the UK government was obliged to honour the Sale and Leaseback for our production and thankfully we went into production on the show; the first series of *The Secret World of Benjamin Bear* premiered in Canada in 2003. Sadly for us, though, the end of Sale and Leaseback for animated series meant that we did not then participate in the subsequent further three series (at a loss of millions of pounds of production that would have made a huge difference to our business) and so we were set back again.

Little did we know then that this was only the beginning of a prolonged period of bad news for the UK animation business.

When The Communication Act 2003 came into effect on the 25th July 2003, removing quotas requiring PSBs to show specific hours of Children's TV, we were still in the midst of production of *Benjamin Bear* and trying to get our newest projects off the ground. We did not really register what the Act might actually mean for us as a business and as an industry. The reality was that it heralded the erosion of the children's public service provision on the commercial channels.

Nevertheless, in the following summer of 2004, we were in buoyant mood. We were going to the Cartoon Forum in Spain with our latest project: a unique and very funny, short-format, animated TV sitcom series (designed using a striking black and white computer graphic style) that would eventually become *The Imp*. And we had a very exciting animated feature entitled *Nocturna*. Feature films *were* still eligible for the UK Sale and Leaseback and we definitely knew how that worked!

Previously we had secured script development funding for *Nocturna* from Scottish Screen (now subsumed within Creative Scotland); and so, with the very talented screenwriter, Philip LaZebnik, we started to work on the script with our partners in Spain and France. The film was looking beautiful: the young Spanish designer/creators were doing amazing work. So it was with a great deal of excitement that I went with my family on a short trip to Bilbao and across northern Spain prior to attending the Cartoon Forum held 22-24 September 2004. There we formally signed the *Nocturna* co-production agreement with Filmax (Spain) and AnimaKids (France). Little did we know that, back home on the 21st September 2004, the UK Government had announced plans for a new film tax credit scheme to tackle the issue of tax avoidance (a subject that had received increasing scrutiny and become a favourite tabloid topic). We had no idea what that might mean for us as an animation production company involved in developing, financing and producing animated feature films using the Sale and Leaseback model… But we were soon to find out.

Things became much clearer in December 2004 when I attended a week-long course in London as part of the excellent 'Inside Pictures UK' film executive training course held within the then UK Film Council's offices. As we sat in session that day, news came in that the Chancellor of the Exchequer, Gordon Brown, had announced the effective cancellation of UK Sale and Leaseback for Film, with no clear date for when its replacement would be introduced. It was a devastating setback for us and, potentially, the project.

That same day, I notified our partners at Filmax that without the Sale and Leaseback financing we would not be able to meet our obligations within our existing agreement. They gave notice of intention to formally terminate the *Nocturna* co-production agreement which I then in turn confirmed to Scottish Screen.

At the time, I still hoped that we would be able to rejoin the project in 2005 because when the new replacement tax credit was announced there was talk of the new mechanism being in place for 2005. We were desperately trying to stay attached to the film and, at the same time, gather as much information as we possibly could about developments within Whitehall. Week after week and then month after month we waited for word of the new tax credit system but nothing came and eventually we had to admit defeat and leave the film. As I look back I know the cost to us as a business was significant: both financially – having invested so much time and resource into the project – and in terms of the lost opportunity. We had been poised to move into a very different type of business and thus grow and develop as a company.

In the end, it would be another two years before the government finally announced the introduction of the UK Film Tax Credit in April 2007: over two and a half years since they had announced its introduction! This delay had a massively detrimental impact on the UK Film industry of which our experience was only a microcosm. And, for those of us whose main source of work was the children's TV business, much worse news was on its way.

By 2006 producers who worked with the children's and animation businesses were becoming much more aware of the need to engage with the politics of policy forming. Within PACT - the UK Producers Association - we understood the need to lobby and to inform. However, one also starts to understand that, when the tide of public opinion goes against you, there is very little you can do to change that. The other thing I have come to understand is that, when it comes to political point scoring, very little scores higher points with the public than issues relating to the wellbeing of children. As a result, kids' TV becomes one of the key battlegrounds for politicians of all kinds, whether within Westminster or positioned outside in lobby groups.

Ten years ago there was an increasing awareness of the impact of obesity and its long-term effects on the health and wellbeing of society. Childhood obesity became the focal point of this debate and within that debate the advertising of 'junk food' to children was viewed by

the increasingly fervid lobbyists as the most visible and easily justifiable of campaigns: an easy win.

Therefore, it came as no surprise when, on 17 November 2006, there was the announcement of a planned total ban on TV advertising to children of HFSS (High in Fat, Sugar and Salt) foodstuffs. Jane Lighting (CEO, Channel 5) commented that "the long-term future of UK-produced children's programming outside the BBC is bleak". She was not wrong in her assessment of the impact that this policy - on top of the previous quota removal and loss of the Sale and Leaseback - was to have on the industry.

Ofcom subsequently announced the advertising restrictions in February 2007, calculating, it was reported, that there would be a loss of £39 million of TV advertising revenue. Ofcom stated that the restrictions "could have a knock-on effect on original children's programming, the scale of which is difficult to determine". In effect the burden of financing children's PSB programming would fall heavily on the shoulders of independent producers.

Further research has indicated that, as the children's television industry argued at the time, the long-term impact was and is far more complex and difficult

to address than anyone wanted to admit: especially those who might be responsible for tackling the problems effectively. The irony is that the very people who see their role and responsibility being the education, entertainment and wellbeing of children through media – children's media production specialists - are the very people who are being undermined by those that claim to represent the interests of children (and for only as long as it suits them).

For Red Kite there was a very clear impact on our business. We had been working with Cromarty based producers Don and Lindy Cameron of Move on Up Productions: initially on an animated series and then on our first ever live-action series, based on the books entitled *Katie Morag* by author/ illustrator Mairi Hedderwick. CITV helped to fund a short pilot, which was shot on the Isle of Lewis, and subsequently gave us a commission to produce a series. However, with the loss of advertising revenue CITV knew that their children's service would not be sustainable in its existing form. They gave us three months to confirm our financing. Previously they would have tracked the project and earmarked the funds, knowing how hard it was for producers to secure finance. Ultimately we had to turn down the commissioning offer and leave the project. It took another five years before the BBC backed *Katie Morag* which has gone on to become an award-winning series. A credit to the efforts of Don and Lindy and everyone involved.

Today it is almost unthinkable that CITV would pay an independent producer to make a programme like *Katie Morag* at the level of funding available less than 10 years ago.

In April 2007 the government introduced the new UK film tax credit, considered to be a significant improvement on the previous Sale and Leaseback structure due to the higher proportion of net proceeds available to producers. The benefit to the UK film industry over the following years was significant with the studios and VFX business in particular seeing a dramatic increase in business volumes. Unfortunately for children's TV and - in particular - children's TV animation producers, there was a continued decline in funding of original PSB programming. Although there were emerging opportunities within the US Children's networks that were subject to a European quota: clearly illustrating the impact of quotas on local content producers.

The pressures of being within a system in the UK that was clearly not working for children's TV production led me to conclude that we needed to do something more proactive: that we had to look for places and opportunities where there was growth. So, during 2010, I started to look at where those places and opportunities might be – focusing on South East Asia. As well as the UK, I had grown up in India and Hong Kong - and also I worked in Asia with HSBC after graduation from university - so I had some familiarity with the region.

In October 2011 Red Kite Animation merged with a newly created entity in Singapore called August Media Holdings [AMH], the intended driver for business growth in Asia and the West. Unfortunately the merger did not work out and after two years I decided to demerge from AMH and start again. So, on the 29th March 2013, Red Kite Animation exited AMH and looked to the future. A future that would include the new UK animation tax credit. But I'm getting ahead of the story…

Back in May 2010 I had been approached by Oli Hyatt of Blue Zoo to join the Animation UK steering committee that had been established to speak up for the specific interests of the UK animation production community. I had been a member of PACT and on the Children's and Animation Group there, on and off, for a long time. With PACT Scotland's help I had set up the Scottish Animation Group and had been part of the efforts to find ways to fund animation via a series of initiatives proposed to government. It was clear to me that a single issue lobby and much broader support base would be far more effective; additional context is that there were some very large beasts in the 'High End Drama' world moving in the same direction and an increasing focus on the creative industries as a driver for UK economic growth.

On 21st March 2012,

Chancellor George Osborne's budget speech confirmed that the lobby had been a successful one, with many people across numerous related sectors helping to secure the inclusion of animation within the UK tax credit. The energy and drive of people like Oli Hyatt, and the support that enabled him to take on the role of champion, meant that we had, from the 4th April 2013, a new source of tax relief based financing in the UK. Oli wrote about the successful campaign in the 2013 issue of this yearbook.

Whilst extremely welcome, and desperately needed as a driver of investment into the UK and into the animation sector, the tax credit isn't the end of the story. The erosion and loss of funding by the traditional public service broadcasters of animated content, and the explosion of digital channels and online providers, means that the prices paid to acquire the content developed and produced by independent producers does not meet the costs of production.

As I sit here at the end of May 2015, poised to start production of our first original series in a long while, I am feeling hopeful that the tax credit and further positive steps in government policy will drive continued growth and development of the UK children's and animation business. As a sector, children's TV sits looking enviously at just about every other genre in television: genres where they receive development funding for their projects and have a clear and transparent tariff structure; and where they are paid properly.

As a Scottish based children's and animation production company, I also wonder where the PSB money that is allegedly allocated for Scottish productions has gone over the past two decades…

I firmly believe that the BBC is one of the greatest media companies in the world and that it has led the way in innumerable areas of our business and should continue to do so in the future. The discussion about the licence fee renewal shouldn't be about if we have a licence fee but how much more could be done with an increased licence fee? As a nation we should back the 'Best of British' companies; we should back the BBC.

Think of the opportunity to increase the funding to the UK children's and animation industry by increasing the allocation of funding to children's PSB across the channels, but with BBC Children's leading the way: setting the standard for fair payments; devolving production and spending responsibilities; supporting the development of UK children's programmes with funding, etc.

The genuine and guaranteed decentralisation of spending to the Nations and Regions would see, for example, BBC Scotland Children's Department given control over the Scottish allocation of funding and becoming a genuine commissioner of local content for a national network audience from local producers. What a difference it would make if the PSBs helped to pay for the development of children's programmes by independent UK producers and then paid a genuine commissioning fee for those programmes.

As I say, I am hopeful for the future. If everyone in our industry and those who care about it engage properly with the issues, and are actively involved, then they *can* make a difference: I have seen this for myself. We need to continue to support those institutions and organisations which have been at the heart of our industry and help them to be better at what they do, so that they in turn can help us to be better at what we do. And most of all we need to keep developing and producing wonderful content for each and every child that makes up our audience. ☺

FUNDING CHILDREN'S ANIMATION IN IRELAND

MICHAEL ALGAR

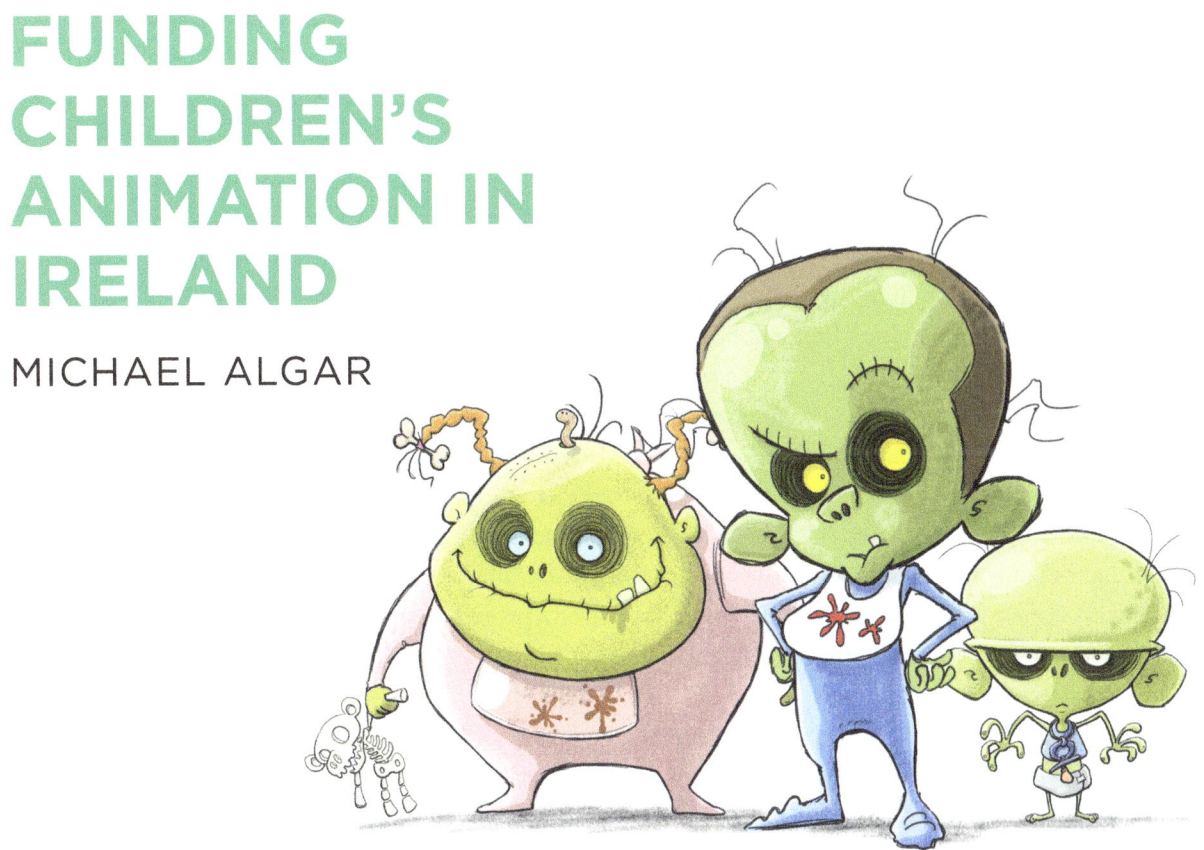

Zombabies © Keg Kartoonz

Although Ireland has a relatively small population for its land mass, its television programming successfully competes internationally due to its high quality and standards, particularly in children's animation. Because of the limited amount of funding available for production, Irish animation studios regularly look overseas for co-producers and international broadcasters who can financially augment what is available locally.

There is a bewildering array of international TV channels available to view in Ireland but there is only a small number of local broadcasters. Of these, TV3 and UTV Ireland don't transmit children's programming, and TG4 largely relies on international purchases dubbed into Irish with occasional licence fees for local productions. It runs children's programming during daytime hours.

The main broadcaster, RTE, is state-owned and dual-funded through licence fees and advertising along with commercial revenue. From its resources it outputs three national TV channels, as well as a variety of radio services, digital outlets, music groups and other utilities. The main TV channel, RTE1, is the national flagship serving the wider population with RTE2 focusing on a younger demographic and having emphasis on sport and comedy while RTEjr is aimed at children aged under seven. RTE2 runs children's programmes during weekday daytime hours and RTEjr transmits 7am to 7pm daily. RTEjr is advertising-free.

RTE produces a large volume of its output inhouse, with a small but growing amount outsourced to independent producers. In the case of children's animation, the financial contribution to independent studios currently averages €500,000 per annum: this typically translates into supporting three or four series. Funding is mainly provided as a broadcast licence fee. In addition, there is a purchasing strategy for completed series which have been funded elsewhere. Commissioned series are initially run on RTE2 and subsequently on RTEjr.

The Broadcasting Authority of Ireland (BAI) operates the Sound & Vision scheme which grants funds for the production of programming which meets certain criteria. To meet EU requirements, the criteria include that programmes must be of high quality and be based on Irish culture, heritage and experience. These factors often prove limiting in attempting to attract international interest in those programmes especially with children's animation which may be consciously non-specific regarding locale. Eligible programme types include animation, as well as live-action drama and documentary. Applications may be made by broadcasters or independent producers. The scheme itself is funded by 7% of the TV licence fee. One of the minimum standards for eligibility is that a programme will be broadcast in Ireland, so that a prior commitment from an eligible broadcaster was a prerequisite but this standard has been reviewed this year and a broadcast commitment may be sought after the BAI has made a decision in favour of a project. On average, the S&V scheme has awarded €350,000 per animation series with typically three series supported each year. Since its inception in 2006, the scheme has contributed almost €10 million in animation production funding.

Established in 1981, the Irish Film Board receives a grant each year for the development of the Irish film industry. With the advancement of the animation sector (mostly children's programmes), the Board has broadened its remit to support television as well as cinema production. Most significantly, the Board is the only state body providing funding for project development. For animation studios this is vital in getting projects designed and written in preparation for pitching to broadcasters and other funding sources. Typically, the Board lends €20,000 to individually selected projects for development although amounts vary.

The Board also provides production funding for selected projects. This in itself represents a validation of the financing of a project, as the Board looks at its commercial potential and international market acceptability. Between cinema and TV, the Board has loaned over €9 million production finance to animation features and series. Film Board funding is provided as a non-recourse loan, with a charge taken over the recipient company.

The most significant source of production funding is the tax incentive known as Section 481. Originally introduced in 1987 as a replacement for the Irish Film Board, it was enhanced and simplified in 1993 when the Film Board was re-established. Designed to encourage private sector investment in production by offering a tax break, it has just been reformed as a tax credit system operated by Revenue. Private investors are no longer involved with one of the results being that most of the costs associated with investment are eliminated.

A production company can

Dependable Dan © Keg Kartoonz

apply for a tax credit of 32% of eligible expenditure incurred on the production of a single project (i.e. a feature or series). The company itself must have been trading for at least twelve months and then have made a corporation tax return – so twenty-one months total. The credit relates to the cost of all cast and crew working in Ireland (regardless of nationality), as well as goods, services and facilities purchased in Ireland. The credit is based on the lowest of eligible expenditure, 80% of the total cost of production of the project, or €50 million (under review). A minimum spend of €250,000 must be incurred and at least half of that must be eligible expenditure.

The company can apply for the full credit on completion, or 90% in advance. If claimed in full on completion, Revenue will pay the credit within 30 days of receiving a compliance report. If claimed in advance, Revenue will seek Film Board or BAI certification, or proof on financial closing that 68% of eligible expenditure is lodged to the project production account, or a tax credit guaranteed by a financial institution. 90% will be paid once one of these three criteria has been met. The final 10% will be paid on receipt of a compliance report. Payment may be claimed against the production company's corporation tax liabilities. If the relief is greater than any tax due, Revenue will

pay the excess. This is a summary of the incentive; there are fine details not noted here!

These four sources of funding together seldom cover the total production cost of a project originated by an Irish animation company. Inevitably, producers look for international broadcasters, financiers and co-producers to work with them in bringing their concepts into production. Animation Ireland is a grouping of companies involved in the sector which specifically promotes its members and their work internationally. It acts as an umbrella under which Irish animation studios collaborate with each other to raise the profile of the country's industry.

ANIMATING THE NORTH WEST OF ENGLAND

PETER SAUNDERS

These are challenging times for producers of animation in the UK, particularly producers of animation for children's television. Falling budgets; audiences drifting away from terrestrial broadcasting; a decline in children's programming on commercial channels; risk averse investors, the rise of gaming and social media; the list goes on and on... These challenges are faced nationally and no doubt internationally but the question I would like to pose is whether the North West of England, which has evolved as a hub for children's animation over the last fifty years, is poised to survive these challenges better than other areas of the UK or is it, in fact, more vulnerable?

The origins of the North West animation industry date back to the 1960s when two young graphics students met at the Manchester College of Art and Design (now the Manchester Metropolitan University). Their names were Brian Cosgrove and Mark Hall.

After graduating from college, both Brian and Mark went to work at Granada Television, which was the commercial television station covering the North West of England at the time. Both worked in the graphics department supplying titles and credits for locally produced shows, Mark even supplying the graphics for Ringo's bass drum when The Beatles appeared on an evening news programme!

In 1969 Brian and Mark quit their jobs at Granada and set up their first company, Stop Frame Productions. The company created both drawn and stop motion animation for commercials, public service films and eventually a children's TV series called *The Magic Ball* followed by the first animated series of *Noddy*. They also produced animated graphics for a Thames TV children's series called *Rainbow*. This was to be their saving grace when Stop Frame Productions hit troubled waters in 1975 and had to close.

Impressed by the quality and professionalism of Brian and Mark - and needing a company to continue the animation for *Rainbow* - Thames Television set the two of them up in a subsidiary company, calling it 'Cosgrove Hall Productions'. Significantly, London-based Thames Television allowed the new company to be established in Manchester. Had Thames insisted that Brian and Mark relocate to London, the scene

we see today in the North West's vibrant animation industry might be very different.

Under the patronage of Thames TV, Cosgrove Hall Productions (CHP) flourished. At the time I joined in 1977, the number of staff had just entered double figures. At the height of the studio's powers in the mid-1980s, over 150 staff worked there producing such programmes as *Danger Mouse* and *The Wind in the Willows*. It was Thames' enlightened view and appetite for animation that helped the company to grow so significantly, and gave CHP three special advantages. Firstly, television was very much a 'closed shop' at the time: you had to have a union card to work in the industry but, in a classic Catch 22 situation, you couldn't get a union card unless you had a job in the industry. This was a real barrier to young people joining the sector, not just in Manchester but the whole country. As a major force in British TV at the time, Thames had the clout to get young talent the necessary union membership and did so routinely. Secondly, Thames liked the animated programmes Brian and Mark produced and wanted more of them in ever-increasing numbers. Thirdly, Thames had the wherewithal to fully finance these

programmes - a state of affairs that contemporary, independent animation companies can only dream of.

So, in setting up their animation subsidiary in Manchester, with Brian and Mark at its head, and by supporting it with commissions and financing, Thames Television played a major part in helping the animation industry in the North West to become established and to thrive.

On 16 October 1991 that all came to an end.

Thames Television was the commercial weekday franchise holder for the Greater London conurbation. Their franchise came up for review in 1991 and, against all expectations, they failed to have it renewed, it being awarded instead to Carlton TV.

Over the course of the following two years Thames Television scaled back their operations both in London and Manchester, eventually laying off all Cosgrove Hall staff and closing the company down.

It's at this point that the animation industry as we now see it in the North West started to evolve. The animation talent that had been nurtured, trained and employed at Cosgrove Hall no longer had a major employer to turn to for work. Small groups of ex-Cosgrove Hall employees set up their own businesses or found employment in other local fledgling companies. Instead of the North West's animation talent being concentrated within one large organisation, the same talent was spread across a wide variety of smaller companies, with more diverse portfolios. It was at this time that Ian Mackinnon and I also set up our own company, the rather unimaginatively titled Mackinnon & Saunders Ltd!

The effects of this diversification, as we can now see with the benefit of hindsight, were pivotal for the growth in the North West animation and digital sector.

In the early 1990s digital animation and gaming was still in its infancy and the sudden influx of animators and designers onto the North West's labour market enabled many of the local digital companies, both game design and animation companies, to take on highly skilled staff that they would have otherwise had to train themselves. This gave them an advantage over digital companies trying to establish themselves elsewhere in the country (perhaps with the exception of London).

Also, traditional, stop motion animation companies such as Manchester based HOT Animation (the production arm of HIT Entertainment led and largely staffed by ex-Cosgrove Hall employees), were free to produce children's animated programmes for broadcasters other than the ITV network, unlike Cosgrove Hall which was obliged to provide programming exclusively for Thames Television. HOT's most famous production is probably *Bob the Builder*, but they also produced other great children's series including *Pingu* and *Rubbadubbers*.

Flix Facilities, now the major post-production house in Manchester, was started by Leo Casserly who was one of Cosgrove's Hall editing team. Flix's body of work is no longer solely related to animation and covers a diverse range of output including television, computer graphics, feature films and programme development.

As for Mackinnon & Saunders, well we've been lucky to enjoy a greater variety of work as an independent company than ever would have been possible before.

So by 1993, although Cosgrove Hall had gone (albeit temporarily), a new animation community had been established in its wake, virtually all of whom, it could be said, shared the same lineage. In fact, after a short hiatus, Cosgrove Hall themselves relaunched, this time with new owners and a renewed sense of purpose.

It can be argued that the events of 1991, unpleasant as they were, actually helped secure the future of the Manchester animation industry and gave impetus to the digital sector. The multiplicity of companies that Cosgrove Hall spawned encompassed a wide variety of disciplines from traditional puppet animation to high end digital gaming, many of which still exist and thrive today, almost 25 years later.

The benefit of having a cluster of sector-related companies is that it enables the formation of a viable, local, freelance pool of talent. Most production companies in the media have project-based work flows requiring them to crew up at the start of a project and scale back on its completion. This modus operandi is standard in London where there are many independent production companies and a large freelance community at their disposal, but it is rarely to be seen in the provinces. The legacy of Cosgrove Hall is that there is now a thriving group of independent producers in Manchester that enables freelance talent to find sufficient work to settle in the North West.

As well as sharing a flexible workforce, there is also collaboration between companies. For instance our own company, Mackinnon & Saunders, recently hired studio space from Factory Create (another local animation company that can trace its lineage to Cosgrove Hall) whilst at the same time Factory commissioned the puppets for the ground-breaking series *Strange Hill High*. This type of close cooperation helps keep costs down and helps maximise production efficiency.

There is also a growing awareness nationally and internationally that the North West is becoming a centre of excellence for animation and digital media, particularly since the arrival of the BBC Children's Department to MediaCityUK. I am under no illusion that Manchester will ever rival London in this respect but whilst the cost of living continues to rise at such an alarming rate in the South East, the North West represents a very cost-effective place to do business.

So why then, if there are all these advantages, could North West England be more vulnerable to the winds of change blowing through the animation industry?

The first potential drawback could be, ironically, the positive effect of BBC Children's move to Salford. At the moment their relocation here has most definitely been a force for good. There has been a marked increase in the production of programmes for both CBBC and CBeebies by North West companies, which is to be welcomed. However, there is always the danger that such an upturn in work could lead to an over-reliance on the BBC, in much the same way that Cosgrove Hall was totally reliant on Thames Television for work.

With the BBC's Charter up for renewal in 2016, and the Government of the day possibly not being the most sympathetic to the organisation, there is uncertainty as to if, or how, our main public service broadcaster might have to change. Despite the BBC's Children's Department being recognised internationally for the excellence of its work, it sometimes feels to me that it is not always appreciated or valued as much as it should be closer to home and it may suffer from unjustified budget cuts.

There is also the increasing threat to traditional terrestrial broadcasting as more people access content through digital platforms. A new model of commissioning is emerging from companies like Netflix and Amazon but it is too early to say how this will compare to the level of programming currently commissioned by the terrestrial broadcasters.

Despite the above, I'm optimistic about Manchester's future as a centre for animation production. And we have greater resilience as a cluster than if we worked in isolation. Companies here are receiving more approaches for commissions from abroad than ever before and more work is beginning to come in for digital-only content.

Brian Cosgrove and Mark Hall started something very special when they formed their first company all those years ago. I doubt they thought that they were founding a new industry for the North West of England but in effect they did and it is still going strong after nearly 50 years. I hope it survives at least another 50! ◡

Note. The views expressed in this article are my own and not necessarily those of Mackinnon & Saunders Ltd.

IT'S ALL COMING BACK TO ME NOW: REMAKING AND REVISITING CHILDREN'S TELEVISION

HELEN WHEATLEY

The idea of a children's classic is one that is familiar to all of us. From the '100 books you must read before you're 14' lists compiled by organizations like the Book Trust, to the endless lists of the best children's films of all time, it is accepted that there are certain story worlds to which we can return again and again, and to which we might want to take our younger relatives.

When it comes to children's television however, are we as willing to install the notion of a 'classic' text? In an era where television circulates easily beyond its initial moment of broadcast (via DVD box set, digital TV repeats, streaming through services like Netflix and Amazon Prime, or even clips of more dubious quality on YouTube), are our children to be encouraged to return to the classics of children's television, or does the constant demand for the 'new' mean that these classics are being too quickly set aside?

This question is partly prompted by the recent slew of remakes of 'classic' children's television: *Thunderbirds Are Go!*, *The Clangers* and *Teletubbies* are all being remade in 2015. Whilst, on the one hand, this signals a healthy industry in which new, big, expensive shows are still being made, it also might be seen as evidence of what Amy Holdsworth (University of Glasgow) calls "the economic 'good sense' of forms of nostalgia television as cheap and populist programming which corresponds with the commercial safety of reproducing past successes and familiar forms". Anne Wood, the original creator of *Teletubbies* recently registered her sadness at her show being remade: "It comes down to the times we're in: people feel safer remaking hits of the past rather than investing in something new... It would be nice if more encouragement was given to new work".

One could understand this commissioning decision if it was apparent that the original shows did not stand up to presentation on the bigger, higher definition, television sets many of us are now watching, but the original *Teletubbies* was being broadcast on the BBC's preschool channel, CBeebies, until very recently (and indeed its contemporary, *Pingu*, is still shown daily). The new *Teletubbies* is to have a "refreshed and contemporary look" according to the BBC, but perhaps it's possible that, in producing such a look, the programme makers might lose some of the allure of the acid-bright play world of the fuzzy aliens.

Maybe then these commissions speak of the nostalgia of commissioners who want to relive the popularity and success of such shows? Is nostalgia always a bad thing though? Arguably, the lists of 'classic' children's cinema and literature are partly inspired by nostalgia for really good stories: for films and books which withstand rereading or reviewing. Thus it is legitimate to add television programmes to this list of much loved texts that we might look forward to returning to in our encounters with a younger generation. Certainly as an aunt, and later as a mother, I relished sharing *The Flumps* with the children in my life, just as I looked forward to reading Maurice Sendak's *Where the Wild Things Are* or watching *The Wizard of Oz*. This suggests that there is real potential for repackaging or rebroadcasting

the classics of children's television, instead of, or even as well as, remaking them for the contemporary child viewer.

In relation to this, Joanne Garde-Hansen (University of Warwick) and Kristyn Gorton (University of York), who are currently undertaking the AHRC funded 'Inheriting British Television' project, illuminate the cultural, social and emotional value of rescreening children's television to wider audiences for the promotion of intergenerational communication. In interviews with the BFI as well as other television heritage organizations they found an acknowledgment of a notable increase in public engagement with children's television if programmes selected, curated and screened promoted the sharing of conversation and memories between generations.

Their work shows that not only does nostalgia pull older audiences to screenings of past children's television but that those audiences use the opportunity to bring their children and grandchildren. This provides a marked opportunity for cross-generational reviewing of television: reactivating a common culture of television that contemporary broadcasters often struggle to create in an era of niche programming and extensive

choice. It makes television inheritable and creates new audiences for archival material.

This same intergenerational audience is also being addressed in the Heritage Lottery funded exhibition 'The story of children's television from 1946 to today' at the Herbert Art Gallery & Museum, Coventry (22 May to 13 September 2015). The exhibition, developed by the Herbert along with Rachel Moseley and Helen Wheatley of the Centre for Television History, Heritage and Memory Studies at the University of Warwick, is an interactive exploration of children's television in Britain, and contains original material from some of the nation's favourite children's programmes. Moseley and Wheatley point out that "the ingenuity and creativity of early television explored in our exhibition lives on in modern children's TV which owes a huge debt to the programming that went before". The exhibition will encourage nostalgia as a more positive force: it is hoped that it will get families talking and encourage the revisitation of the classics of children's television.

KIDS' TV:
IS THAT ALL
THERE IS?

SIMON PARSONS

There was an old lady who lived in Liverpool in a house she shared with three sisters and a brother. Out of eight children only three had married. The rest lived together in the tidy house with green gates and a neat privet hedge.

Often on a Saturday a young lad called Anthony would sit and sip from one of those big china cups that you had to balance in a saucer, the kind of cup that, back in his house, only the adults used. But at Auntie Liz's house you were trusted.

"Pick a treasure!" she'd tell him and Anthony would gaze at the ornaments that gleamed on the polished window sill or the sideboard or the mantelpiece. "Ah the Mexican Dancers..."

and so would begin another adventure, just an old lady and a boy and two cups of tea. Quite how old she was was hard to say because if anyone ever asked, she'd tell them she was 4000 years old.

Teacup Travels, which aired for the first time on CBeebies in February 2015, is the brainchild of Anthony Bibby, a little boy who used to sip tea from a china cup, who grew up, built an advertising agency, sold it and now works as a consultant. His mum still lives in hope he'll get a proper job, like many mums do.

A lot of us probably miss the targets of our mother's ambitions but grandparents and great aunts often have the wisdom to avoid the mistake of painting too detailed a picture of the future. They have the gift of being more objective and more fanciful all at the same time: an ability to open the door to a world where rules are merely guidelines. That's not to say that parents are all rule-bound disciplinarians or that all children have the perfect relationship with the older generation, but that kinship one step removed is sometimes endowed with a kind of magic.

Thanks to the nurturing support of CBeebies and our friends at Creative Scotland, what began with that house in Liverpool and a collection of ornaments would become a TV series with a catalogue of museum pieces. Auntie Liz became Great Aunt Lizzie thanks to the extraordinarily gifted (and BAFTA winning) Gemma Jones, and Anthony became alternately Charlotte and Elliot. The series is successful in its own terms and the future is an open book. But it is something else too.

For Anthony, for my partners at Plum Films (Micky and Tina) and me, it is now business; and for a group of people it was the labour of love that paid their mortgages last summer. You work for the money of course you do, and if you make a profit you can keep going and make another show; and so on we go making shows for kids in a world far different to that which Anthony, and I too for that matter, grew up in. Time presses in on parents in a land where now people from all over the world live in a great rich tapestry, but where families are so extended kids often have no connection with those outside the nuclear circle; where street games are unthinkable and even the pavements have been co-opted by adults as improvised car parks. Great Aunt Lizzie's world is a thing of the past, so alien to many modern British kids it's another world. It's why *Teacup Travels* looks so old fashioned; so unrealistic it's believable.

I first read about the house on College Road nearly four years ago. When we began pulling the threads of the *Teacup Travels* team together we had no idea we'd end up with a BAFTA winning top actress, still less a double Oscar-winning production designer (step in Leslie Dilley). It happened because they were enchanted by the old lady from the house with green gates.

To begin with the stories had been fantasy tales about pirates and dinosaurs but somewhere along the way we came to the idea Liz would have more mystique if her ornaments were real ancient artefacts. If it turned out she really was 4000 years old she could even have picked them up back when they were just bric-a-brac. Historical fiction for CBeebies? And not only were the objects genuine so was the woman.

Liz was a woman who pushed at the boundaries of a conservative world with only a glint in her eye to betray the mischief she concealed beneath an otherwise conservative surface. Whether she was 4000 years old or not she was certainly an adventurer as all the photographs of her testify: astride a motorbike; standing in China on an ornamental garden bridge (or was it the winter-gardens in Southport?); even draped in the arms of a mysterious stranger. There are values in her world, some of them old-fashioned, but at the bottom of it all are some things about children some modern adults forget.

When Anthony and his screen cyphers Charlotte and Elliot take a sip of tea and head off

into the adventure Lizzie evokes with nothing more than the power of words, they are not - as some Facebook comments have it - telling adults in faraway places how to behave. For a brief moment they *are* adults, coming face to face with grown-up challenges, in the safety of Lizzie's kitchen over a cup of tea.

And what about that tea? It's funny the number of people who've had a quiet chuckle. "What's in it?" Like so many things we say about children it reveals more about the commentator. Children don't need crutches to help them leave behind another grey rainy day and roll off into the world of their imagination. Give them the power of suggestion and you can't hold them back. A wooden camel gets up and heads away across the cushion sands. An ornamental plate is a raft tossed across the carpet sea. And if they are lucky enough to know an old lady who claims to be 4000 years old there is no limit to where they can go.

So we turned Auntie Liz into Great Aunt Lizzie. We wrote 25 historical fictions and sent an invitation to a nation of kids to head for the museum. (The fictional Lizzie's collection is scattered from Inverness to Exeter with Belfast and Swansea and Durham and London and points in between.)

As for the real Liz, she, like most of that generation born in the early years of the twentieth century, has gone forever. The house with green gates was sold long ago and all that remains is a collection of ornaments split between a group of adults who remember an old lady telling stories while they sipped from a china cup.

It is likely that, in a hundred years, all this stuff we all make - week in, year out - will be nothing more than data sitting on a massive drive in an unfathomably vast 'cloud'.

But is that really all there is?

Time is precious and in the space where the Great Aunts used to be, there is sometimes us. And if we are lucky enough to be on their screen as they lift a cup for a sip of juice, we'll transport them off on an adventure. And if they happen to share it with an aunt or a grandpa, they will remember. The next story you tell might be the one they remember for the rest of their lives. 🌐

CHILD AND YOUTH PERSPECTIVES AND RESEARCH

OFCOM'S MEDIA LITERACY RESEARCH ON CHILDREN'S CRITICAL AWARENESS

ALISON PRESTON

To what extent are children aware of how search engines operate; how they are funded; what and where ads are positioned? How do they decide which content to trust online and how much trust to they tend to give to different sites?

As children's lives become more enmeshed with online activity, these questions become more pressing than ever. It is increasingly important for them to be able to 'navigate knowingly' through the media they consume and interact with and to make informed choices about the content and services they use.

Ofcom has a statutory duty to promote media literacy which we carry out through the provision of research and its dissemination to a wide range of stakeholders. In 2014,

our *Children and Parents: media use and attitudes report* interviewed 1660 children aged 5–15, and 2391 parents of children aged 3–15. We carried out some in-depth qualitative research examining how children thought about issues of risk and trust. We also began, in 2014, our *Children's Media Lives* qualitative longitudinal study, which follows the same 18 children aged 8-15 for three years. This article sets out Ofcom's research findings in the area of critical awareness.

Before turning to the issue of how children think about the information they receive and seek out, it is useful to start with a reminder of what they are using for such information sources. In our 2014 survey we asked 12-15 year olds to say which of the (prompted) sources they would use for various types

of information: "serious things that are going on in the world"; "fun things like hobbies and interests"; and "how to build, make or create things". As Figure 1 shows, for serious things, over half of them nominate the BBC, and one in five Google.

For fun things, one third nominate Google, followed by a quarter saying YouTube and one in five social media. For 'how to' information, YouTube was used by one third, as was Google.

The importance of the BBC as a news source was underlined in our qualitative research, with many children citing it as their main source of news information. This was due to a range of factors including its position as a key 'offline' brand, and reinforcement from parents and from school that this was a brand they could trust.

The use of Google was also

Figure 1: Online sources of accurate/ true information among 12-15s

QC48A-C

I'm going to read out some types of information you may want to find out about and I'd like you to say which one of these you would turn to first for accurate and true information online about...

(prompted responses, single coded)

Base: Children aged 12-15 who use the internet at home or elsewhere (584 aged 12-15)

Source: Ofcom research, fieldwork carried out by Saville Rossiter-Base in April to June 2014

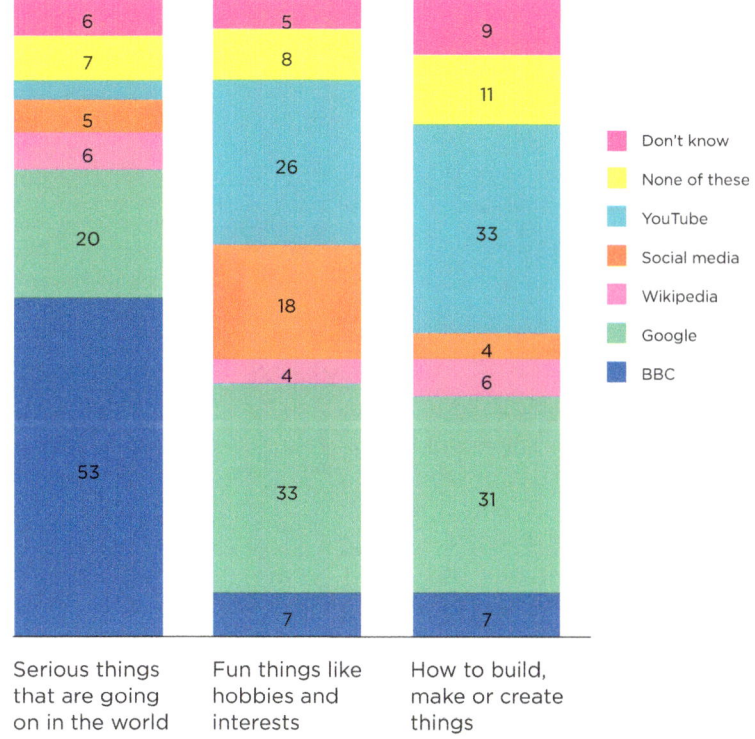

Legend:
- Don't know
- None of these
- YouTube
- Social media
- Wikipedia
- Google
- BBC

	Serious things that are going on in the world	Fun things like hobbies and interests	How to build, make or create things
Don't know	6	5	9
None of these	7	8	11
YouTube	5	26	33
Social media	5	18	4
Wikipedia	6	4	6
Google	20	33	31
BBC	53	7	7

Figure 2: Understanding of paid-for results returned by Google searches, among 8-15s who use search engines

QC30

Here's an image (SHOWCARD OF IMAGE) from a Google search for 'trainers'. There are three results at the top which are in a shaded box. Do you know why these three results are shown in a shaded box?

(Spontaneous responses, multi-coded)

Base: Children aged 8-15 who go online at home or elsewhere and use search engine websites or apps (396 aged 8-11, 530 aged 12-15).

Source: Ofcom research, fieldwork carried out by Saville Rossiter-Base in April to June 2014

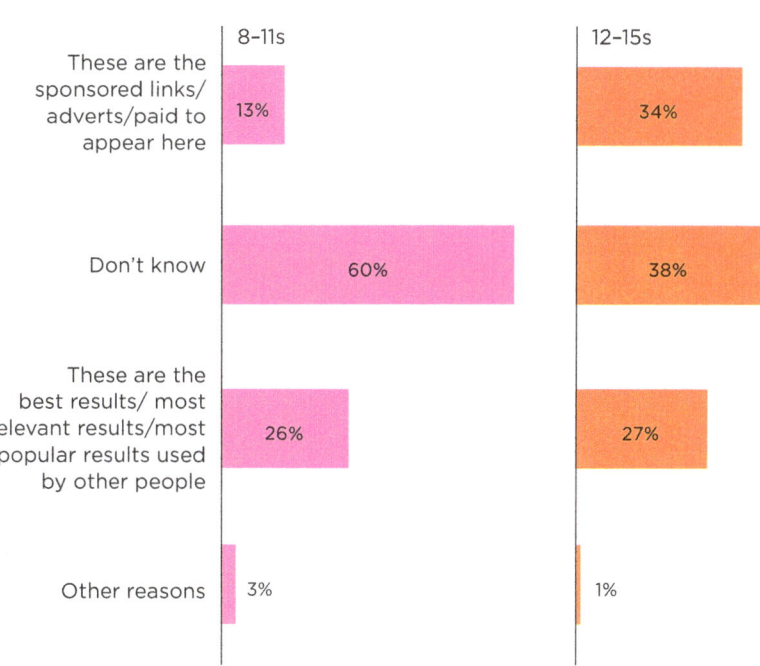

	8-11s	12-15s
These are the sponsored links/adverts/paid to appear here	13%	34%
Don't know	60%	38%
These are the best results/ most relevant results/most popular results used by other people	26%	27%
Other reasons	3%	1%

Figure 3: 12-15s' understanding of results listed by search engines, 2014-15

QC28A

Which one of these is the closest in your opinion about the truthfulness of the information in the websites that appear in the results pages?

(prompted responses, single coded)

Base: Children 12-15 who go online at home or elsewhere who ever use search engines or apps

(313 aged 12–15 in 2009, 503 aged 12–15 in 2011, 479 aged 12–15 in 2013, 530 in 2014)

Significance testing shows any change between 2013 and 2014.

Source: Ofcom research, fieldwork carried out by Saville Rossiter-Base in April to June 2014

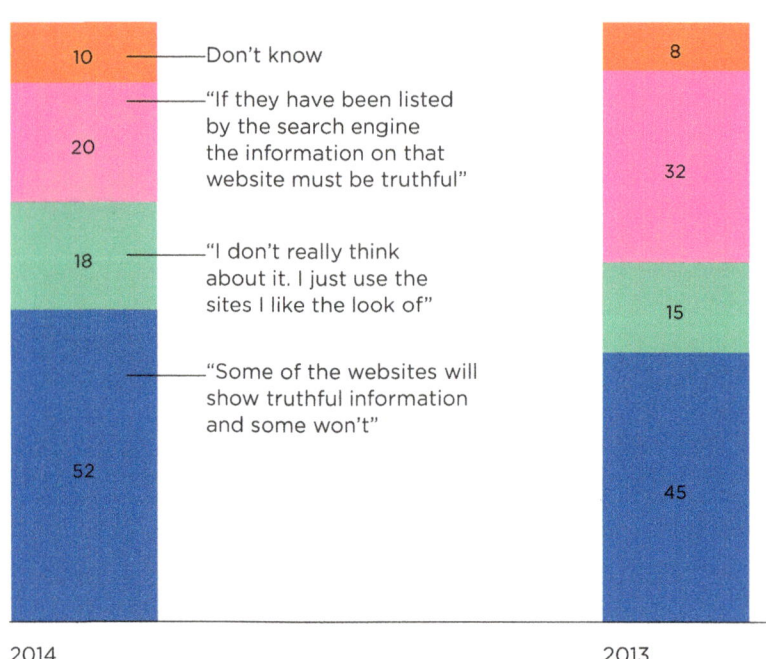

ubiquitous in our qualitative research, across all age groups, and children of all age groups placed considerable trust in it:

"I just use Google. I'd just rather use it because I'm used to it. I think Google is more trusted. On most computers, you can go straight to Google."
10-11 year old boy, Leeds

We also have a range of survey questions that assess the extent of understanding that children have about the search engine, to gauge how far they are aware of its means of funding; how far they are aware how to distinguish between advertising and editorial; and the extent to which they understand the

basic function of a search engine as an aggregator, rather than providing a gated editorial stamp of approval.

As Figure 2 shows, children aged 8-15 have a limited understanding of why the paid-for results appear on a Google search results page (at the time of the survey, these were represented by a shaded box at the top of the page). One third of 12-15s who use search engines correctly said that such results were sponsored links or ads, but only one in eight 8-11s knew this. Six in ten 8-11s didn't know the answer, and four in ten 12-15s. And around one quarter in each age group gave the wrong response, thinking that they were

the best or most popular results.

Qualitative research from our *Children's Media Lives* project provides further insight into the extent to which children were able to identify advertising. It found that for most of the children, TV adverts were the most recognisable as 'advertising'. Any online video adverts, such as those at the start of a YouTube video were therefore also relatively clear to the children. Many of the older children were also aware of adverts that 'pop up' on websites or are embedded in the website content. However, even in these fairly straightforward examples it was rare for the children to know the basic

Figure 4: Children's belief in the truthfulness of websites used for school/ homework

QC18B/A

When you go online you may visit [TYPE OF WEBSITE]. Do you do this? IF YES - Do you believe that all of the information you see is true, most of it is true or just some of it is true?

(prompted responses, single coded)

Base: Children aged 8-15 who use the internet to visit relevant websites at home or elsewhere).

Source: Ofcom research, fieldwork carried out by Saville Rossiter-Base in April to June 2014

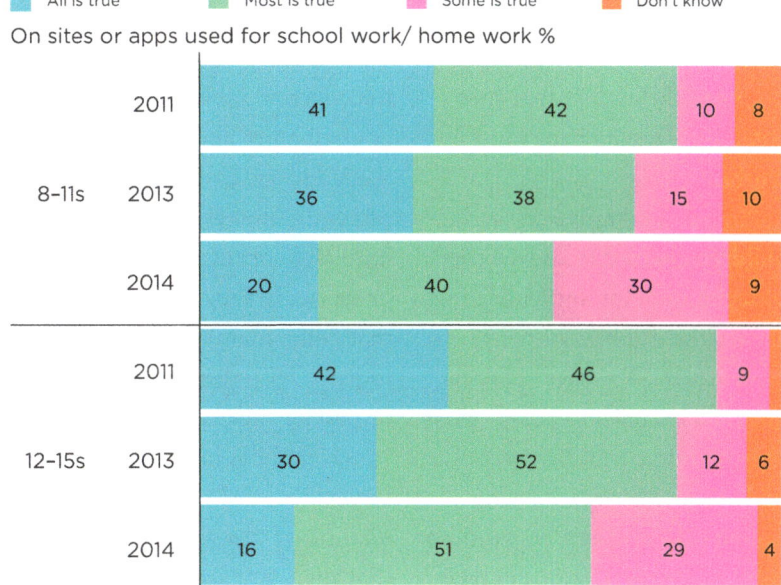

On sites or apps used for school work/ home work %

- All is true
- Most is true
- Some is true
- Don't know

8-11s
- 2011: 41 | 42 | 10 | 8
- 2013: 36 | 38 | 15 | 10
- 2014: 20 | 40 | 30 | 9

12-15s
- 2011: 42 | 46 | 9
- 2013: 30 | 52 | 12 | 6
- 2014: 16 | 51 | 29 | 4

business model underpinning the adverts, and that the channel or site displaying the advert would have been paid to do so. When prompted about why the adverts might be there the children came up with some creative responses.

> Moderator: 'Do you know why the Disney Channel might have adverts and CBBC might not?'

> Nadia: 'I think because the Disney Channel, if it's a movie, you have to take a break, because if it's filmed right now they might be exhausted.'
> Nadia, aged 9

Many of the children, particularly the younger ones, also mostly failed to notice many of the less traditional kinds of advertising, with in-game advertising, product placement and personalised advertising almost completely invisible to them.

In our survey, we also ask 12-15s about the truthfulness of the information they get back from a search engine results page. They are asked which of the following statements they agree with:

"I think that if they have been listed by the search engine the information on the website must be truthful."

"I think that some of the websites in the list will show truthful information and some will show untruthful information."

"I don't really think about whether or not they have truthful information, I just use the sites I like the look of."

As Figure 3 shows, around half of 12-15s give what is the critically aware response: that some websites will be trustworthy and some won't. One in five say they don't really think about it, and a further one in five think that "if they have been listed by the search engine the information on that website must be truthful". This latter group are therefore particularly at risk, as they assume that the sites they visit are going to be some kind of safe environment given their status of being returned by the search engine.

It is useful to note, however, that since 2013 there has been some improvement in children's understanding in this area, with a reduction of twelve percentage points in their belief that sites listed on a results page must be truthful.

In our qualitative research, children claimed to use a variety of techniques for authenticating the trustworthiness of online information. Younger children aged 8-11 tended to accept what they had been told by parents and school about managing online risks and as a consequence were relatively cautious in their approach. 11-14s were more inclined to take more risks, not least as part of their overall development as new teenagers, and therefore their behaviour tended to belie their level of knowledge. Older teenagers tended to place more importance on trust than their younger counterparts, borne out of their earlier experiences.

Overall, children tended to know that it was important to cross-reference between three different sources – although it was unclear how often they actually did this in reality. They tended to rely upon the look and feel of a site, upon whether or not it was a major (offline) brand and upon parents and peer recommendation. It was

also of note that they tended to think that video material was intrinsically authentic – that the camera didn't lie. They were also very clear about the commercial motivations of companies and brands and tended to see companies as therefore unlikely to provide unreliable or misleading content or services. They tended to think that companies would not want to jeopardise their businesses by providing such content.

Over time, however, from the evidence of our surveys and qualitative research, it appears that there are some signs of increased critical awareness or media savviness in relation to children's belief in the information they encounter online. We have asked the same question since 2011 to 8-15 year olds about the level of truthfulness they find on websites or apps "used for school work or homework" and "about news and what is going on in the world". As Figure 4 shows in relation to the former, children aged 12-15 have shown a decreasing tendency to say that "all" the information is true across both areas, and rising proportions opting for "some".

This brief overview of Ofcom's current research on the topic of critical understanding

and trust in information illustrates some increase in levels of awareness that not all that is online is truthful and safe. However, given that 92% of online 12-15s say they use search engines, and, as we saw earlier, 20% of this age group would go to them first to find out accurate and true information about serious things that are going on in the world, the level of understanding about what is an advertising message on such sites and what is not should give us food for thought. In addition, there remains considerable unawareness relating to various other forms of advertising and funding, leaving children potentially vulnerable to some types of advertising, for example product promotions on social media.

Clearly then, critical understanding skills are important. Children need to develop 'media savviness' alongside their increasing consumption habits. Doing so will keep children safer online, increase their digital competence in line with their confidence and reduce the risk of negative online experiences. ◔

CHILDWISE: MONITORING THE CHANGE

JENNY EHREN

The 2015 CHILDWISE Monitor Survey reflects a changing landscape in children's digital media consumption. For starters, more kids now own a tablet than a laptop and more 11–16 year olds can upload a picture to the internet, than can boil an egg. CHILDWISE have been studying media consumption and purchasing behaviour among children aged 5-16 for more than twenty years. We have tracked the rapid growth of the internet and subsequent connected technology and we have watched closely as an online ecosystem has emerged, permanently changing the way in which children and young people consume media.

It is now easier than ever to access information, as well as to share content with peers. Mobile technology has made communication more convenient whilst also transforming the humble mobile phone into a sophisticated hub of information and entertainment. Our technology has become 'smarter', allowing more and more devices to connect to the internet – whilst content is continually refreshed and can be accessed anywhere, at anytime. Nowadays, most children have never been a part of a world where the internet is not omnipresent – and as a result, they engage with technology differently.

> "I basically live on the internet. It's just amazing. But if it goes down e.g. my router stops working or there's high traffic, then I just cry inside."
> Boy, age 15

> "The internet is my life, I literally love the internet. Whoever created the internet deserves a prize because they are super cool. It makes me happy and helps me connect with people who I wouldn't be able to talk to if it wasn't for the internet."
> Girl, age 11

> "It's the new generation of communication and fun. But it can cause more trouble than it's worth sometimes e.g. Facebook, Instagram, Twitter..."
> Girl, age 13

CHILDWISE Monitor data illustrates how children's media use is in a process of continual change. Traditional television viewing is declining and internet use is rising. Mobile phones are becoming increasingly pivotal among older children, whilst tablets dominate the attention of younger children, despite only gaining prominence in the last few years. Households have transformed since Monitor first began, from having just a television set, to having four or five different devices: PCs, mobile phones, laptops and now tablets have all become commonplace, with some of the older gadgets now declining.

In 2015, the majority of children now have their own computer or tablet, phone, games console and television – but console and television ownership is falling and phones are static, though more of these are now smart phones. Tablet ownership continues to grow although this too is slowing. Parents have thrown their weight behind tablets because they are controllable – a tablet can be given or taken away to reflect good or bad behaviour, in a way that is not possible with a conventional television set or computer. Apps can be purchased as rewards, and, with the growing use of tablets in primary schools, there are perceived educational advantages. One in three children aged 5-7 now have their own tablet: double the number recorded a year ago. For older children, where patterns of technology use are already established, the tablet is slower to displace existing allegiance to a laptop or smartphone, especially among teens. Mobile phones are increasingly used for internet access and are the main way of listening to music among older children.

> "My tablet is my favourite because I love to play on all my apps and go on YouTube. Otherwise it would be my TV but I've got BBC iPlayer already so it would be pretty boring because my tablet's got games, YouTube and more."
> Girl, age 11

> "I can't live without my iPad because I can FaceTIme people on it, message people on it, listen to music on it, go on the internet, watch things on it, go on my apps e.g. Instagram, Snapchat. I cannot live without my music and social network sites"
> Girl, age 12

> "I have tried not watching TV for a day but I couldn't, I was soooooo bored. So I just have to have it because it entertains me"
> Girl, age 10

> "I love my phone and without it I feel like a nobody."
> Boy, age 14

> "My mobile phone is barely out of my hand. I use it a lot just on social media such as WhatsApp, Snapchat, Facebook, Instagram etc."
> Girl, age 15

> "I've got so used to coming home doing homework and going on my games console that it just wouldn't feel right without it. Also I wouldn't know what to do with myself as my parents would be on their tablets and there is nothing on the TV."
> Boy, age 13

> "I love my xbox, I always play it. I would rather have fun playing online on Call of Duty: Blacks Ops 2 with my friends, than watch TV all day"
> Boy, age 12

With traditional television viewing in decline, children have drifted away from mainstream television channels, in favour of paid for on demand content, via services such as Netflix. The majority now watch TV via alternative devices, though the television set is still the preferred method for most. However, television should definitely not be written off prematurely, and there should be no doubt that it still plays a very important role in the media lives of children. The resurgence of *Hollyoaks*, *The Big Bang Theory* and *EastEnders*, and the enduring appeal of *Friends*, have given it a greater focus in the last year, while cult series such as *The Walking Dead* and *The 100* catch the attention of older children.

But as new technologies come and go, the fundamental principles of *what* engages children remain static. Children will always look for an element of play and entertainment in any new technology or media they adopt. This is evidenced by the two biggest hits from last year: YouTube and *Minecraft*. Both are linked with the further rise of tablet and smartphone ownership among children and the trend for internet access to emulate the ubiquity previously enjoyed by television. TV viewing still occupies the greatest amount of their time but internet use is steadily closing the gap.

YouTube is the top favourite website for boys and girls across the age range, displacing Facebook among all bar the oldest girls. Two in three children visit each week. Past concerns about the risks of encountering unacceptable material on YouTube have largely disappeared, with parents of even the youngest children now happy to let them use this to access their favourite television programmes, music, games, demos and vloggers. YouTube is increasingly the place where they will go to search out information and online material; in the same way that Google Images superseded Google as the search portal of choice, YouTube has now taken this a step further.

By contrast, *Facebook* has long lost the primacy that it enjoyed a few years ago. It remains a must-use utility for most older children, but now sits alongside Instagram, Snapchat, and to a lesser extent Twitter, as a place to keep in touch and share experiences with friends. The growing popularity of vloggers, such as Zoella and Alfie Deyes, is in part an extension of this diffusion. These sites give teens a chance to tune in to the thoughts and antics of others not so dissimilar to themselves, and feel part of a wider community (which is reassuringly hard for adults to comprehend).

Minecraft is widely popular for boys and girls across the age range, with children engaging across a range of channels and equipment: playing the game on computers, tablets, consoles and smartphones; watching demo videos on YouTube or uploading their own; talking to friends as they play; and also reading the growing range of print manuals and other books that feature the game.

Part of the initial attraction, especially for older children, has always been the sense that this is a collaborative and user-directed game, comparatively non-commercial by today's online standards and with an anarchic slant. It is a game that each user can adapt to their own personal preferences, encompassing design and building, challenge, competition, communication, and much more. However the user profile is becoming ever younger, and the recent sell-out to Microsoft has been greeted with concern by some hardcore users, worried that commercial imperatives will change the game.

Despite the ever-increasing use of the internet and modern technology by children across all ages, the printed book continues to hold a place in their lives. There are signs that print, alongside other old technologies, is fighting back and adapting to ensure survival. Most children read books for pleasure, although only a minority do so every day, and children's titles have seen great success this year. Seven out of the ten top selling titles across the market are children's titles, and an eighth - Guinness World Records - is largely aimed at this age group.

Links with internet, film and television are key drivers. Four of these top titles are *Minecraft* manuals, plus the latest books from David Walliams (well known from TV), Jeff Kinney (Wimpy Kid originated as an online series), and young adult writer John Green (*The Fault in Our Stars*, released as a film last year). These three writers have another ten titles between them in the top one hundred. Vloggers Zoe Sugg (Zoella) and Alfie Deyes both had books in the top thirty as well.

Recent trends indicate that over the next couple of years, children's use of the internet is likely to overshadow the time they spend watching television. Traditional TV viewing continues to decline at a steady rate whilst hours spent online will increase. The internet enables children and young people to seek out their own content and as such, we expect the use of on-demand services such as Netflix to become a routine activity. We also expect Smart televisions to be widely adopted, further enabling children to find the programmes they want to watch rather than be restricted by linear television listings.

In the next five years

The next five years could mark a period of convergence for the technology that is currently in use. The recent release of the 'phablet' – a mobile device designed to combine or straddle the form of a smartphone and a tablet, could become a popular gadget for children and young people. Televisions are likely to be internet-connected in some format, allowing for the streaming of content from portable devices to the big screen, whilst Cloud technology will further encourage an environment where children and young people will expect to be able to access their files and information anywhere and on any device.

In the next ten years…

Looking further into the future, children will have little understanding of a world without the internet. The 'internet of things', a concept in which many household objects communicate and share data using Wifi, could become an accepted norm – whilst having appliances which cannot be controlled using a smartphone or some kind of online dashboard may be seen as dated and old fashioned. Wearable technology is likely to have progressed significantly by this point. Most children will have some form of wearable tech., be it a smart watch, smart glasses or a virtual reality headset. Whether these devices will be used to the same degree as mobiles and tablets currently remains unclear.

Magazines have failed to emulate this resilience however, with sales and readership falling year on year. Apart from football magazines among boys, this year's only success is Marvel, acquired and relaunched by Disney and capturing readership among girls as well as boys. The ephemeral nature of magazines makes them an easy target for the wide range of internet sites that offer similar material, often for free, for any child who chooses to look online. Sharing a magazine in the playground or on the school bus has given way to pocket games, music, or sharing posts and pictures on social media via their mobile phones.

As we move into the future, there can be little doubt that children will continue to spend more and more time on the internet, particularly as growing numbers acquire devices that are 'always online', such as smartphones and tablets. Connectivity has become a fundamental need for young people, and whilst this remains, there is little sign of the technological revolution reaching its end.

Our latest report – Connected Kids , highlights the progressions of the last twenty years, using past data to make predictions on how children will interact with technology in the future. To the left are some of the themes that we believe are likely to emerge in the coming years.

1   CHILDWISE Monitor Survey – a comprehensive annual research study with more than 2,000 children and young people aged 5-16, across the UK. The study looks at children's media consumption and purchasing behaviour, and at aspects of their wider life. Children are interviewed via the CHILDWISE schools panel http://www.childwise.co.uk/reports.html#monitorreport

2   CHILDWISE Connected Kids Report – highlights the progressions of the last 20 years, using past data to make predictions on how children will interact with technology in the future. http://www.childwise.co.uk/reports.html#specialreport

THE TEENAGE WORLD OF MEDIA

SOPHIE EDWARDS

Media, in my view, is all encompassing. I find that you can waste hours on an app with it feeling like mere minutes. The super availability of media is affecting how we think and feel about things. I only use certain social media: Instagram, BBM, YouTube, Spotify, Shazam, BBC, Buzzfeed, Netflix and Duolingo along with photo editing apps. Personally I do not use simple addictive games such as 'Flappy Bird' or 'Crossy Road' since I'm too busy!

About two or three years ago I began watching YouTube videos and it made me realise how similar you are to people. For example these YouTubers, who were just normal people in Britain, had the exact same sense of humour as me. Originally I thought you would have to be older to get some of the humour. Maybe knowing that adults and children aren't so different made me mature more quickly.

Through YouTube and other social media sites like Facebook, I find that you compare yourself to people a lot. Through media you can sculpt your life as you would like it to be seen. For instance you would never post a picture of yourself crying on the sofa or when you've just woken up with bedhead. So, especially if you are young and naive, you might compare your 'boring' life to that of more 'exciting' strangers you will probably never meet. This is definitely a negative approach to media but it should not be ignored.

I have come across many online shops selling homemade arts and crafts. I think this is such a nice way of using media to your benefit. Even teenagers are selling their art over Instagram and I find that pretty amazing.

A lot of my friends don't watch TV anymore: it has been replaced by phones and tablets. Rather than sitting watching TV you will find yourself talking to friends and browsing through people's lives when you're on the couch. You can never get bored.

At the moment I am trying to spend less time on my phone because it has made me less of a productive person; I wonder what I would've done in that one hour I 'wasted' on my phone. However, I believe once our generation is older, we will all be too busy to spend as much time on our phones.

Media is growing with my generation and I feel in the future there will be apps I wouldn't even believe possible. Obviously I have considered the negative future - everyone on their phones, nobody actually talking face to face - but I do think this is very extreme and we as a human race couldn't cope with those conditions.

It's important to remain aware of the bigger picture though and watching BBC news on morning TV whilst eating breakfast isn't enough to stay informed. I *know* that there's so much going on in the world that I'm not aware of. Whilst my parents get their news from the website and occasionally inform me, I still feel I am yet to engage with media in a more considered way. I feel media is an ever-changing and unassailable entity. I can see it, I can reach it, but it only exists as far as I perceive it.

THE NEW AGE OF MEDIA

JOSIE KELLY

As a self-proclaimed television addict from about the age of two, I feel I have appropriate qualifications to analyse and critique the media platforms given to the British public. With technology changing day by day, this rapidly moving, media-fuelled environment seems all a bit too alien for many: yet, as an eighteen year old, this new technological revolution we are all currently a part of feels bizarrely normal. I can't NOT state the obvious and leave out the fact that the progress in technology has advanced our communication abilities to what, even ten years ago, would have seemed unimaginable: be it hashtags or instant video messages, people of all ages have instant connections to one another globally. This could be argued to have facilitated the crazed online fangirling of hit TV shows such as *Pretty Little Liars* and *Keeping Up with the Kardashians*, as we now have instant access to shows broadcast across the Atlantic and immediate contact with fellow obsessive fans via Twitter and other social media platforms. Each discovery made of a new social media website or app seems to just slot into our lives and somehow manage to break the mould and overtake Facebook for its brief ten months of fame. Remember BBM? Well that was one social 'hype' that came crashing down once the (for now) seemingly untouchable iPhone conquered the now historical Blackberry.

Twitter has become such a massive part of everyday life for so many - from politicians to school children. It seems everyone has Twitter and it has become the must-have media tool to stay informed with just about anything that's going on. If you have not yet followed the crowd and conformed to the Twitter way of life you are merely limiting your own knowledge on things happening both nationally and internationally. I could bet the hashtag '#MENINIST' will mean absolutely nothing to those who don't have Twitter. Whereas all my fellow tweeters were able to view millions of tweets made by the thousands of unheard men across the UK voicing their sarcastic, under-appreciated (and deeply concerning) worries such as "Why are the fattest women the biggest feminists?" So if you haven't got Twitter I would advise you to straight away go and sign up and judge for yourself what the issues (and the issues *behind* the issues) are.

As media has progressed, so have our humours and interests, goodbye memes and hello vines. We have formed a culture of video nerds, all we want is to be humoured via moving images. A man dressing as a woman and pretending to be his own girlfriend? Classic. A lone boy walking up to strangers and sniffing them? Hilarious. And the best? A turtle singing to Coldplay. Absolutely brilliant. Every day members of the public are constantly able to break the internet and make their mark: so step aside Kim K, we have a laughing goat on our hands here. This new way of finding fame and building careers has proved successful to many yet also caused problems for others; there is something rather unsettling about watching a video published to provoke laughter at a stranger's misfortune in outfit choice or a slip up during a drunken night out.

I have so far failed to discuss television and its importance in the contemporary media world; not because it's become less significant or because it doesn't have a vital role in society today, but because I think, as media has adapted, television has managed to keep most of its originality. Programmes broadcast to the nation have always held huge amounts of responsibility as they have constantly challenged people's beliefs and brought to light issues others are facing across the world. The new forms of media have only improved this way of reaching out to people and draw public attention to the massive problems faced by millions globally. To discuss every implication surrounding the current technology we have access to this would require too many dissertations! However in the main I feel if you are able to use the new media abilities we have *wisely*, anyone can have an impact and this is what is fantastic about the broad and holistic platform future generations will grow up surrounded by. It gives ordinary people a voice, bringing power back to the citizens who not so long ago may have felt a little unheard. All you need to do is look at the online feed during the recent build up to the 2015 General Election and see people's passion light up online: we may love our 'thug life' cats and dancing sheep but they're not the only things that get us tweeting. ☺

GROWING UP IN A DIGITAL WORLD

FLORA WILSON BROWN

In 2014, 94% of American teenagers aged thirteen to seventeen reported going online daily, and 34% said they were online "almost constantly", according to Pew Research Centre. Most teenagers have one or more social networks and this kind of instant access to the lives of our nearest and dearest (as well as hundreds of acquaintances) must have an effect on how we interact with the world.

One of the biggest problems with growing up in a fully digital world, as far as I can see, is that every stupid, rash or hurtful decision you make is documented forever. Adults who got to grow up before the internet (and especially before Facebook) were far more free to make bad choices; of course there were consequences, but there was no danger of a potential employer seeing a picture of a messy night out or arguing with your friend and being confronted with a complete transcript the next morning. Now, every mistake you make is up for discussion by your entire social circle and it makes it a lot harder to just let things go or fade into a rose-tinted memory, because you're faced with the stark evidence of reality on-screen.

Ironically, in contrast to my previous point, another big

problem with digital media is the ability to become anonymous, one of the crowd, completely absolved of responsibility for your actions at the click of a button. Mob mentality has moved off the streets and onto the internet; just two minutes of scrolling on the comment section of any website is enough to obliterate any faith in the kindness of strangers. Women, especially women of colour, have to deal with huge amounts of online abuse ranging from explicit and often sexual threats to derogatory comments about their appearance. Even if misogyny is increasingly unacceptable in real life, it remains prevalent online, which leaves me wondering how these men interact with the women in their lives, whether they would be happy to show their mothers these comments. It is a little scary, knowing that any of my friends could be online, in disguise, spewing hate. But this isn't just a fixture of the online age, more a symptom of a long-standing issue in our society. Often, it seems, social media doesn't create problems but unfortunately provides a platform for ones already there.

However, I do consider social media to do more good for society than it does bad. I'm very often told by my dad and people in his generation that the rise of technology has killed communication, but I really can't understand that viewpoint. Teenagers are *constantly* in communication: we talk all the time to friends who live in the same town; friends who moved away; and (most importantly, I think) friends from right across the world. One of my best friends lives in Florida, we've never met face to face but I talk to them every day on Facebook, instant messenger and Skype. We share all the same interests and know everything about each other's lives yet we're told that we're not 'real' friends by people who are still in touch with their childhood pen pals, or have reconnected with them on Facebook (in a wonderfully ironic twist.) Of course, if we could see each other in real life, we'd jump at the chance, but the fact that we can't, whilst annoying, doesn't affect how we feel.

Another complaint aimed at social-media-savvy teens is that we don't care about real issues. I can see where one might get this impression, as scrolling through a constant stream of consciousness is not always the most politically thrilling or testing experience. But social media is proving an incredibly important platform: the Ferguson protests and the blacklivesmatter hashtag are excellent examples. Young people are taking a platform designed for communication and using it to its full potential, and spreading ideas and raising awareness of injustices that often go unnoticed. Teenagers don't always trust the traditional media (newspapers, TV and radio) to tell them the truth so they have created new forms: tweeting information; taking pictures or videos; and livestreaming events as they happen. They act as journalists on the scene but, instead of taking hours or days to produce the information, it takes seconds, minutes, before the whole world can see. The recent General Election blew up my Facebook timeline as people shared articles, choice parts of the manifestos, opinions, and yes, photoshopped pictures of Ed Miliband. It's less that today's teenagers don't care about important issues and more that they engage with them in different ways, often involving photoshop, capitals and a lot of swear words (the last two being tried and tested teenage methods of protest, of course).

My final point is a more personal peeve and possibly not a view you will have come across on the subject, so bear with me. I love selfies. I really do love them. I love it when my friends post them, because it means they feel so happy with their appearance that they want to show everyone. I love seeing strangers' selfies on Tumblr, because I get to see people I'd never see otherwise; and I love taking my own, because it means I have a record of how I looked as a teenager and it makes me feel confident. Naysayers have such a hatred for selfies you'd be forgiven for thinking we were bringing about the end of the world, instead of taking a couple of slightly pretentious pictures.

But, in a culture where it is easy to make people feel bad about their appearance and to encourage them to buy beauty products (the recent 'beach body' advertising campaign scandal being a pertinent example), taking a selfie can feel like a very small act of rebellion telling all those companies that you are good enough and you are worth showing to the world, just as you are. Whilst selfies may have been popularised by social media, it's useless to pretend that the human race hasn't always been in love with its aesthetic image; today's selfie is yesterday's expensive portrait and we have whole museums dedicated to those (not that I'm suggesting my selfie belongs alongside a Holbein.) And really, in amidst all of the hurt and terror in the world, I do struggle to believe that teenagers posting pictures of themselves is the worst thing we face as a society.

I spent a lot of time considering whether growing up in a digital world has made my generation markedly different to those raised before and I'm not sure I've come to any firm conclusions. Of course, I have nothing to compare my experience with: I can't remember a time without the internet. That said, I don't think the internet has made us any better or any worse as people: I think we're exactly the same as humans have always been, but now our experiences are amplified and performed on a (potentially) massive public stage. Some people choose to use this platform positively, to make new connections or start movements for change. Others choose to use it negatively, to post anonymous abuse. And I think it's just that - a choice. Growing up in a digital world comes with all the same choices as we've always had but now the whole world is watching us make them. I can only hope we get it right. ☺

HOW ARE TODAY'S TWENTY-SOMETHINGS ENGAGING WITH DIGITAL MEDIA?

MEGAN NICHOLSON

The older generation often wonders why people of my age are constantly on their mobile phones. But whether it is watching a vlog on the way to work, creating a blog, or following their favourite celebs and industry professionals on Twitter, this is just the average day of a twenty-something year old with an interest in media convergence.

We begin our day by checking our smartphones, we end our day by checking our smartphones, and we check our smartphones throughout the day! And to the dismay of many fifty-somethings, we can easily pick up on one device from where we left off on another which makes us a technically savvy generation.

Almost all twenty-somethings in the UK own a smartphone or table device, enabling us to surf the net all day long and avoid the real world, watch television on demand, and have tomorrow night's little black dress ordered and easily delivered right to the front door (avoiding those overheated shopping centres that we used to love as teenagers). Simple.

Digital media acts as a convenient social aid for our age group. Allowing us to comfortably watch TV from anywhere (as long as we are connected), listen to the radio or podcasts as we jog to the gym, and use something as small and mobile as a smartphone, to become engrossed in the trends and goings on around the world.

Media platforms such as Facebook, Twitter, Instagram, and Tumblr are the majority of this generation's way of hearing about and sharing news. We are able to like, repost and share anything as trivial as how hungry we are feeling, to how fantastic the last audition of Saturday night's *Britain's Got Talent* was.

When we actually do watch linear TV, it mainly consists of time filling. E4 programmes like *How I Met Your Mother*, ITV's *TOWIE*, or unique Channel 5 documentaries such as the recent *Freaky Eaters*, are usually viewed whilst we slob out with nothing else better to do, or they simply serve the purpose of being background noise.

But on the whole, people of this age consume television in a way that suits them: at a time when they have time. iPads and apps such as BBC iPlayer, Netflix, ITV Player, Amazon Prime, and TVCatchup are all popularly used, enabling us as the audience to choose what we want to watch, and more importantly *when* we want to watch it.

It could be argued that twenty-somethings engage with television in this non-linear way as they are simply not available at the times when the programmes are originally broadcast. This could be for many reasons: work or study commitments, or, for some, even sleeping arrangements. People of this age tend to structure their routines around what suits them. But, it can also be said, that people of this age have very varied tastes.

Some like to be cultured whilst enjoying documentaries, or be educated and entertained by programmes like *QI*. In comparison, others like mundane entertainment that can be found within a stream of daytime TV shows like *Jeremy Kyle*, *Judge Rinder*, or *Countdown*. Alternatively, a vast proportion of this age group, prefer to 'get into' a series on Netflix and 'binge view' rather than waiting to watch episodes week by week, like the rest of the population.

This age group is known for having high tech skills in downloading films and series, as this is thought of as a free way to consume TV. Although the BBC is a public service broadcaster, making its content free to view (but funded by the licence fee), people of this generation seem to be less interested in the mainstream and more interested in the up and coming: the YouTube vlogs, the short-form clips, the whatever-will-be-next platform.

I would argue that today's twenty-somethings are the first born members of the digital generation. We are of the age whereby we were young enough to adapt to the changing consumer trends that occurred as we grew up. The childhood cereal box treats of tacky toys have now become treats of gaming codes to add to your online profile. And the change within digital media consumption is even more apparent in our altered demands of Walkmans to iPads for Christmas; from Gameboys to smartphones for birthdays.

Therefore, it is evident within our constantly tweeted, Instagrammed, and shared world, that online we are releasing more and more information about ourselves. The stream of our light afternoon snack photos, and the process of how easy it is to access, upload, and share YouTube content suggests that people of this age are constantly conscious of the digital media world around them. We feel the urge to keep the world up to date with each of our daily activities through the use of bizarre hashtags.

#whateverwillbenext. 🙂

THE PHENOMENON OF CELEBRITY VLOGGERS

JOHN CHISHAM

Vlogs, video blogging, what does it all mean? Your kids know.

Let's go back in time! It's the 17th century. The Globe Theatre is England's highest form of entertainment, offering joy to the five and a half million inhabitants of England and Wales who might visit. Flash-forward to the 21st century and the YouTube 'vlogger' Tyler Oakley has over six million subscribers. This essentially makes him Shakespeare.

This is completely barmy!

Tyler Oakley, a mortal man of just 26, has more people following him than the entire population of England and Wales in the 17th century! Let's put this into perspective. If Tyler Oakley and the entirety of his subscribers were to travel back in time to 1066, they would outnumber the assembled armies at the Battle of Hastings six hundred to one. Seriously, if Tyler Oakley commanded all of his viewers to start wearing their shoes on their heads a large amount of parents would simultaneously ask the question "Why are you wearing your shoes on your head?" and chaos would ensue.

It's intriguing when you acknowledge how long digital technologies have actually been around for. We have barely scratched the surface of the potential of online media. YouTube was created in 2005, meaning it has only existed for ten years. Ten years! The younger generation can't imagine a time when videos of celebrity vloggers and funny cats dancing to 'Gangnam style' aren't just a click away. The growth and success of 'celebrity vlogism' certainly didn't happen overnight, but in all honesty, it didn't take much longer than that.

Eight years ago, Charlie McDonnell, an ordinary teenager living in Bath, posted vlogs on YouTube to an audience of barely 100 people. Then, literally overnight, his comedic video skit, 'How to get featured on YouTube,' featured on the YouTube homepage. In the space of mere hours, the subscriber count of his YouTube channel 'Charliesissocoollike' was boosted from approximately 150 to 4000. As the channel began to mature, the subscriber count only increased, becoming the first UK YouTube channel to reach a million subscribers and building to two million by May 2013.

What's that you say? "Charlie McDonnell is now a fully grown man. He shouldn't be making silly YouTube vlogs anymore!" Well that would be a silly thing to say. Presumably as a result of a deal with YouTube and then Google, McDonnell can earn revenue from making his videos. This is now his job. He is a YouTube vlogger. Yes, in the modern world, people can have careers like this.

Similar to the likes of Spiderman, 'with great power, comes great responsibility'. Like Oakley, McDonnell is at the helm of a mighty mass of viewers. Young viewers especially. His actions and behaviour in his videos can influence the actions and behaviour of thousands if not millions of his young, stereotypically impressionable, viewership. Luckily, McDonnell is a decent human being. McDonnell's charity collaborations with the likes of Cancer Research UK and UNICEF are impressive given his youth, and subsequently show the next generation his vitality to invest in helping others. Surprisingly, McDonnell achieved all of this without being bitten by a radioactive spider, thus making Spiderman look like an uncharitable fool.

What I find intriguing is that Charlie McDonnell has no obligation to keep his viewers updated on his life. He could easily just quit YouTube and work as a baker, or postman, or whatever he may please. However, he continues to vlog. The loyalty and trust that has been created within his fan base is astonishing. Most of his viewers are growing up alongside him, experiencing the transition into adolescence together. There's something reassuringly humble about that.

We might also want to consider Toby Turner aka 'Tobuscus'. He is described as an 'internet personality' and has created an enterprise of content across his three YouTube channels: 'Tobuscus', 'Toby Turner' and 'Toby Games'. It's fair to say that he may be a workaholic. On his secondary channel 'Toby Turner', Turner vlogs everyday, rambling about his exciting new projects; his participation in mundane activities; and any other thoughts which pop into his head. Toby's charisma and random humour never fail to make me chuckle.

Turner produces regular comedy sketches and animated parodies on his main channel. However, he keeps the attention of his audience through daily vlogs on 'Toby Turner' and videos of him commentating whilst playing video games on 'Toby Games'. Turner certainly produces a quantity of content, and in the world of celebrity vloggers, quality isn't always necessary.

With a similar subscriber count to Tyler Oakley, Turner is able to sell merchandise of his 'Tobuscus' brand to his fans, thus generating more revenue.

There is another side to

celebrity vlogism which is the casual vlogger. An example of one of these would be 'MorganPaigeLoves'. This chirpy, sarcastic vlogger has cultivated a niche audience of just less than 35,000. Being inspired by McDonnell a few years ago, Morgan was slightly late to jump on the 'hype' of celebrity vlogging when it first appeared. Her vlogging is not a career, so, in all probability, she likely has a *real* job. This means she hardly qualifies to be a 'celebrity' vlogger. However, I feel that this vlogger has a healthier relationship with her audience. Her audience understand that she's a real person and not a character in a TV show or film. Morgan is often open and honest in her videos which usually consist of humourous anecdotes of her daily life and experimental filmmaking.

There is no pressure to appeal to her subscribers or churn out content like some sort of freaky cyborg vlogging machine as per the previous vloggers I have mentioned. To me, her videos seem honest and truthful, thus highlighting how each vlogger has a distinct personal style.

Though some vloggers on the internet actually have very little that's creative to say. They are just ordinary people with an audience, like a dog barking into a megaphone in the middle of the street - it's just annoying.

With the exception of politically-minded vloggers such as Russell Brand, the tone of celebrity vlogs are usually quite light-hearted. It feels as if you are having a very one sided conversation with an upbeat, friendly acquaintance.

People can become utterly consumed by this. Celebrity vloggers: are they your friends? Watching their vlogs on your tablets or phones in the comfort of your own home can provide a close relationship between viewer and vlog-content provider. There's a personal intimacy to the proceedings. You invite the vlogger onto your screens, and in turn they invite you into their lives.

Twitter has further narrowed the gap between the viewers and their idols. In a sense, the internet both distances the audience and the creator, yet brings them ever closer together. It's not a big scary company producing these videos: it's usually just one 'real' person.

As the actor Kevin Spacey so philosophically put it during his speech at the 2013 Edinburgh Television Festival, "actor, writer, producer, director, these kids on YouTube can be all these things". Spacey suggests that YouTube, the internet and the ability to vlog has provided creative freedom. This allows artists to create whatever content they want, publish it online, receive feedback and even generate an audience - all for free! The phenomenal thing about celebrity vloggers is that both creators and audiences are active, purely producing and consuming content that they want.

Vlogging is new. It is freedom. It brings people closer together. There may be a screen between one another, but that doesn't make the relationship any less genuine.

MAKING 'I AM LEO' – CBBC'S FIRST FILM ABOUT A TRANSGENDER CHILD

CAT LEWIS

"We're all humans, we all deserve to have acceptance in this world. I'm proud of me being trans. I'm proud of my gender and I want every other trans person to look at themselves and say, 'I'm proud of who I am. Yes I've had rubbish back in my life, but it's made me the person I am today.' That's how I feel."

These words never fail to move me, even though I've heard them so many times. They're delivered from the heart by fourteen year old Leo as part of the video diary he made for 'I Am Leo', a documentary my company produced for CBBC's *My Life* strand. Teenager Leo lives as a boy, but was born in a girl's body, and the film we made with him is the first programme commissioned by CBBC about a transgender child .

Lyndsay Rowan, who works at Nine Lives as an Assistant Producer, came up with the idea, having read Leo's story in the newspapers. He is one of the first children in the UK to be prescribed hormone blockers to prevent the advancement of puberty in the gender he doesn't identify with. I've made other documentaries with adult transgender people, and I know how hard it is for them to reassign their gender

once they've gone through puberty, so I wanted to make a programme illustrating this new, alternative treatment pathway. Transgender children are more likely to be bullied and also to self-harm or attempt suicide – all very important reasons to make a film. Documentary is a great medium through which we can educate people about medical breakthroughs and widen the circle of compassion. Also, children aren't born with prejudice, so by helping them understand difference at an early age, I genuinely believe we can make the world a better place.

When we first approached CBBC commissioner Kez

Margrie with the idea, she was understandably very wary. She very much wanted to commission a film about a transgender child for the *My Life* series but had to be sure that the child and their family were robust enough to cope with the long-term impact of the film. Television programmes are now immortal thanks to the internet, so it's more important than ever to ensure no damage can be caused to vulnerable contributors as a consequence of appearing in them. However, despite Leo's youth and our duty of care to him, we knew he was just as passionate as we were about telling his story. Even more importantly, we knew his mum Hayley was very supportive and firmly believed her son should make a documentary with us.

We talked to Kez about our confidence in Leo and his family. We also arranged for him, his mother and his sister to talk to a child psychotherapist about every aspect of making the film for CBBC, which included her finding out if they were likely to cope with being targeted by online 'trolls'. The fact that Leo had already told his story in national newspapers and on ITV's *This Morning* made it easier for CBBC to seriously consider commissioning the film, because the main facts were

already in the public domain. The channel wouldn't be the first to reveal Leo was born a girl and, because he'd already gone public, CBBC felt confident that he and his family were strong enough to cope with the consequences of sharing his

secret. Kez decided to seriously consider the idea and we made a taster to show just how strong a communicator Leo is. We all felt the universal theme for the documentary should be the need we all have to find our identity and be accepted for who we are.

Once 'I Am Leo' was commissioned, we thought through the natural boundaries that come as a result of making a documentary on this subject for children. I see such editorial boundaries as positive, because they force you to think more creatively. I always employ filmmakers who are full of good ideas about how to make the best possible programme but more importantly, I need to know they will always put the long-term welfare of our contributors first at each stage of the production and beyond.

I chose shooter/producer/director Phil Niland to make 'I Am Leo' because he is a very sensitive and experienced filmmaker. Also, as a gay man, Phil can relate to Leo's desire to clearly communicate his identity to the world; he knows what it's like to grow up in a minority and he also had to deal with bullies in his youth.

We ensured we included in our documentary the important fact that, at his primary school, Leo had felt bullied and misunderstood not just by pupils, but also by staff. His family had contacted a charity called Press For Change who helped resolve the issues.

We wanted to work closely with the Tavistock & Portman Clinic during the making of the documentary, to ensure we could film Leo being treated and capture on camera detailed answers to our questions about giving children hormone blockers. We also wanted the clinic's staff to act as consultants for our documentary, to ensure it was totally accurate at each stage. However, the Tavistock has refused virtually every request to film for the last twenty years, due to the sensitive nature of their work and because, understandably, their staff were determined to put patient welfare first. It took real persistence over many months for AP Lyndsay Rowan to win their trust and cooperation. We were all so pleased Lyndsay achieved this, because it gives our documentary real credibility. The Tavistock is thrilled with the final programme, which they describe as "ground-breaking", and their staff now show the documentary to other children and parents considering hormone-blocking treatment, as do other gender identity clinics.

Trust built on positive, honest and constant communication is the key to maintaining close relationships with all contributors, particularly those at the heart of a documentary, and Lyndsay is excellent at this. As an Executive Producer, I deliberately hold back, because the immediate members of the production team need to be the ones forging and maintaining these relationships during the production. I always meet the contributors towards the end because I usually help record the commentary, and then as a company, we maintain constant touch with all the contributors we've made films with.

Our commissioner Kez Margrie is herself a BAFTA-winning filmmaker, which is one reason she's great to work with. She's very creative, and always suggests good ideas that improve films. With this documentary, Kez came up with the final title 'I Am Leo' and she pushed us to find a strong narrative arc. It's always incredibly important for a documentary to have a forward driving narrative, to ensure it has a beginning, middle and end. Without this, however strong the contributors and the subject matter, there's no compelling reason to stay watching. The typical narrative arcs used in documentaries about transgender adults are to follow them through surgery or through their gender transition. This wouldn't have been appropriate for us given our audience, but even if it had, Leo had already been taking hormone blockers for six months when we started filming and he had lived as a boy for years, so there wasn't a natural narrative arc for us to follow there. After talking at length with Leo and his mum, Lyndsay found out he had defaced his current passport because it labelled him a girl and that he hadn't yet applied for a passport as a boy. We all felt following Leo's journey to get a new passport as a male would give us a strong narrative arc that was a very a relevant way into his story for children. The only obstacle we faced is that it took the family a very long time to find his existing passport, so we could show on camera how he'd defaced it!

We wanted to be accurate, clear and sensitive about how we explained to viewers why some people are born transgender and how hormone blockers work. Phil Niland came up with the main animation idea of a production line in a factory dropping male and female brains into stick people. We could then explain visually how sometimes male brains are dropped into female bodies and female brains end up in male bodies. We also wanted to visualise how hormone blockers work and our editor Brendan McCarthy came up with the clever idea

of adding an umbrella to the animation. As a team leader, it's really important to create an environment in which everyone is inspired to contribute at each stage of the filmmaking process, because the more engaged the team is, the better the final film! Phil also came up with the bright idea of 'pausing' the actuality of a chat we'd filmed between Leo and the head of the Tavistock Clinic, to reveal how hormone blockers stop working as soon as someone comes off them.

My company Nine Lives was first noticed in 2009 when we made a one-off documentary for BBC Three called 'Small Teen Big World'. It was a film about 15 year old Jazz Burkitt who has a form of dwarfism; it attracted very high ratings as well as critical acclaim. The producer/director Kerry Brierley made the ground-breaking creative decision to ask young Jazz to record the commentary. This immediately made the documentary, about a young disabled woman, empowering, sincere and intimate. We went on to make another five films with Jazz for BBC Three using the same technique and when we started making documentaries for CBBC in 2012, it was natural for us to want to use the same technique. It was undoubtedly harder, because when we made

'Me, My Dad & His Kidney', our main contributor, Raphael, was just 9 years old and I had to bribe him with toy soldiers to get him to finish recording his commentary! It was worth it, because the documentary immediately felt like a film *by* a child *for* other children, and it won a BAFTA. We've always asked the contributors in our CBBC documentaries to voice the commentary since and it works, as it does in 'I Am Leo'.

As Leo was older, we also left him a video camera during the whole production period and it was AP Lyndsay's job to regularly nag him to record his video diary. We ensured he reflected on camera after each filming day, but we also asked him to use it when he just felt he had something to say. He knew Lyndsay and Phil were going to go through his video diary, and kept telling them his entries weren't worth watching. Thank goodness they didn't listen and instead carefully looked at everything, because that's how we captured his wonderful statement quoted at the start.

FEAR AND LAUGHING

ANGELA SALT

Illustration by Stuart Harrison

"Laughter is the shortest distance between two people." Victor Borge, comedian, pianist.

A funny thing happened to me in early childhood. My mother, suffering from postpartum psychosis, pushed my pram in front of a double-decker bus. A Tupperware Lady saved my life. Susan, a perma-permed seventies heroine rescued me and afterwards gave me a plastic giraffe. 'Party Susan' I think of her, aptly named after her Tupperware 12" divided snack tray. She had a laugh so distinctive it whoops through the decades and I can hear it still... She was funny and sing-song and good at telling stories. I spent a lot of time round at her house with a giggle of bad-haired children pretending to be The Bay City Rollers on a band break, watching *Basil Brush*. When my little sister spent months in a gloomy, Victorian hospital 'Auntie' Susan helped look after me and was cheerfully reassuring, assuaging my fears with her funnies. Susan's Tupperware plastic beakers were *always* half full. She was warm-hearted, optimistic and naturally comic.

Why do I want to write comedy for children? Because I think growing up with a good sense of humour is vital, and funny feels like sunshine. THE best sound in the world is children laughing. Better even than a theatre packed with commissioners laughing, I believe, or else viral YouTube videos of Heads of Acquisitions 'ROFLing' would be 'a thing'.

As a writer I regard myself as fortunate in being able to draw upon my utterly dysfunctional childhood. "I can smile about it now but at the time it was terrible" as Morrissey sang with The Smiths fifteen years later, crashing the charts with their own double-decker bus story. I'll spare you the worst of it but on the *brighter* side there were power cuts; I was terrified of dogs; my two budgies died in a brutal cage fight; I broke my arm pretending to be *The Bionic Woman*, Jaime Sommers, jumping off a swing in slowmo; and I had the 'ugly' Sindy nobody wanted with the short, Brillo pad hair and a chewed foot. Creepy prints hung on the walls of my home: the allegedly cursed 'Crying Boy' in my bedroom and two infants perilously close to an unguarded, open fire in the living room. I was basted with oil to burn in the 1976 sun. The lurid clowns on my bedroom wallpaper came alive at night and choked up sausage strings – wait, I might have imagined that one...

But to take my young mind off all that there were *The Clangers*, *Crystal Tipps and Alistair*, and *Crackerjack!* I was GLUED to the telly as a child and I stuck the (oh so carefully unpeeled) yellow cellophane wrapper off a Lucozade bottle over ours to make it 'colour'. BBC One aired a great new sitcom for kids, *Here Come the*

Double Deckers! (everybody *of a certain age* in the kids' industry seems obsessed by that show, even those for whom double-decker buses hold no especial meaning). I don't hold the Beeb accountable for my post-traumatic flashbacks: I'm the only adult I know who still waits for the green man. Every. Single. Time. Unfortunately I was sent sprawling by a cab carrying Paul Daniels and his lovely wife, Debbie McGee in Soho a few years ago re-carving those mental scars. I didn't bother suing, I could imagine their defence lawyer going, "So, what first attracted you to step into the path of millionaire Paul Daniel's oncoming taxi?"

While I'm here (nervously watching oncoming traffic) I'm really perturbed by kids on phones on kerbs these days... Thank heavens there are cartoon videos like "Dumb Ways To Die" that they can watch on their phones on kerbs now. We need more of this sort of thing: terrifying warnings wrapped up in an earworm. I LOVE writing earworms. I wrote a whole bunch called, "Don't Lick Your Pets" for a YouTube Series which sadly never got to air. The current pet population stands at 65 million in the UK including fish. Well, fish don't stand but I don't see anyone else addressing

this pet-licking issue – not even 'animal lover', Ricky Gervais.

Our three children, Marlin (16), Mathilda (13) and Austin (8) have no pets, sadly, after I refused to get them a phoenix on fire safety grounds. They are however growing up in a household with access to twelve screens and we all know the internet was invented for LOLcats so they can have those instead and be grateful for fewer asthma attacks. I'm thankful that there's a world wide web and multiple channels of funny content available for my kids to enjoy and that commissioners seem to have an insatiable appetite for comedy – Hurrah! We can EAT, children! (NB comma there.) I try hard to amuse them myself but the two teenagers give me that head-tilted, slack-jawed, dead-eyed look like condescending, freshly-caught cod when I try to joke, especially in front of their friends. They don't tell anyone what I do for a 'living'. Last week I even overheard my young son explaining to his friend, "My mum stays at home all day but she rarely cleans. She's on her computer a lot, on Facebook I think." Marlin, the eldest, is in the eye of the GCSE storm right now and is way more stressed than I was sitting 'O' Levels. My own friends are reporting their teens especially are increasingly strung out too and it's a widely held belief that social media's cranking up the pressure on them and adding a multitude of complications we didn't have to deal with growing up. On the one hand it's positive that they're able to share their thoughts and concerns so readily and immediately, but if that just leads to unresolved co-ruminating it can make a difficult situation worse. Of course kids need sensible, responsible support and guidance through their problems but sometimes it's good to try and persuade them to see the funny side too. How many of us have distracted a grazed child with a giggle? It works with emotional hurt too, in my personal experience.

Children are now living and developing dual identities: one in the physical world and an alternate digital reality; and there are increased peer pressures and dark online places only clicks away. I was horrified recently to discover that Tilly was being 'followed' by individuals promoting pro-self-harming and pro-suicide websites on Instagram after she altered the privacy settings (that I'd set for her) from private to public so she could accumulate more followers. It was naughty - I'd only agreed to let her

use Instagram privately - but she wasn't fully aware of the implications. Luckily I was on it fast and closed her account down as a consequence. We had to go over why it's so crucial to be careful online. It's harder these days for children to escape exposure to real world horror and atrocities and as a parent that worries me. As a content creator it makes me even more determined to give children plenty of positive, life-affirming FUN content.

I try to write from a child's perspective and from the heart even if that means recollecting my own childhood fears which are imprinted in full sensory detail. I don't see that as a negative: on the contrary I think it helps me to be empathetic as it's like a shortcut straight back to the experience of being small. I think having been an anxious child makes for very vivid, enhanced recollection as I was hyper-aware of so many details in my physical world and also I had an overactive imagination! It's common for children to have everyday anxieties and phobias: to have nightmares and be afraid of what lurks under the bed, in the wardrobe, in the wallpaper, in that dubious pasta sauce masquerading as ordinary, plain 'red' flavour... It's even scarier when adults are

blithely oblivious or dismissive of the *obvious* extreme peril. My sensitive boy, Austin, now aged eight, was really concerned by something he saw in a cartoon two years ago:

"You know mum, I don't think young children should watch Looney Tunes because they show walking in the sky and that could encourage them to walk in the sky and fall down and actually die. Tell the people you know who make cartoons that."

It made me laugh but he was being dead serious and I assured him that I'd pass his grave concerns on, so CONSIDER YOURSELVES TELT, you 'people who make cartoons'.

I'm serious about making children laugh because it's very important work. According to latest figures from the Office of National Statistics, 10% of children in Great Britain aged between five and sixteen have a mental health problem, with 4% of children suffering from an emotional disorder such as anxiety or depression. I know first-hand that laughter is a great and reliable tool for dealing with adversity in life. There are physiological and psychological benefits to laughing. Laughter diminishes fear.

I'm currently developing and writing *Bear, Bud & Boo* - a

brand new, adorable animated comedy for Technicolour, aimed at children aged four to seven - in which one of the main characters is nervous and beset with anxieties. Through this character I intend to shine a light on common childhood fears – of the dark, separation, loud noises and so on - but hopefully help to dispel them because in the context of the character they're very funny. When children can laugh at what scares them the fear loses its potency. I watched my trypanophobic (needle-phobic) thirteen year old have a canula inserted on laughing gas last year so I *know* that for a fact. It was totally hilarious for her, albeit bizarre for me!

When I'm writing a comic character (any character for that matter) I always imagine their fears in great detail because they spur that character to behave in a certain way, they're a key (albeit often hidden) catalyst for action. Fears fascinate me because they're so often surprising, idiosyncratic and *funny*. Prior to Austin's first school trip to a safari park when he was four he brought home a letter which asked parents to note any anxieties their child might have:

"Do you have any fears I should tell your teachers about?"

"Yes. Tell Mrs Tickle I have *two* fears. Lions ... and ... um...

PEACOCKS!"

This was news to me. Peacocks hadn't featured in his first four years as far as I was aware... I won't allow their feathers in the house. They're *very* bad luck!

What I do allow in the house is copious cartoon watching. I believe I am doing the very best for my children letting them spend uplifting hours watching Cartoon Network. This is completely scientific: laughing feeds brain development by increasing blood flow to the brain. My kids don't play the flugelhorn or mudbath ballsports at some ungodly hour on a Saturday morning, but I will insist they get up to watch cartoons with me at least for an hour or so, no matter how much they protest they have homework to do. It's what Saturday mornings are made for in my opinion. The eldest is in MENSA so it obviously hasn't been too detrimental. Marlin made an interesting point, actually, while we were all enjoying *The Amazing World Of Gumball*, which was that, "it's so cool to have something we can all watch together, something that's genuinely funny, not adult or sweary or rude." Approaching seventeen she still likes animated shows which are ostensibly for children but can be appreciated

by a wider audience, because they give her something to discuss with her much younger brother apart from, "Why do flies eat poo?"

It's great when, as a family, we can find something which makes us all laugh together which is age appropriate from eight to forty-six. Comedy which connects us as a family is a joy to find. And it's increasingly important for us to carry on bonding when generally our family media consumption habits have become more fragmented. We subscribe to Sky and Netflix and we have a Nintendo Wii, Smart TV and fifteen social media accounts between us. I want the children's media community to keep coming up with ace content to make my kids swarm on the sofa together with me and their dad (even though trying to squeeze five onto a three-seater is guaranteed to cause a temporary kick-off!). It's just jolly nice being in close proximity even if the kids *are* all second-screening and I'm covertly Facebooking on my iPhone under a cushion... Of course these days, whoever's sitting the shortest distance from the router has the last laugh! ☺

FAREWELL

KATY JONES
1963-2015

BARNEY HARWOOD

So, it's around three years ago: a Sunday morning around 8am.

I had been travelling through the night on my return journey from another *Blue Peter* challenge and had managed about three hours sleep in the car park at Keele Services.

I knew I had a full day of filming to look forward to; I knew it was for BBC Learning and I knew I was meeting this lady, called Katy.

I also knew that the constant twitching in my left eye wasn't going to look too good in the close-ups!

I met Katy at the front door of the location "Good morning, Barney! I hear you've had a long journey?" she said with that lovely 'mum smile' thing she did, then she reached to the table behind and passed me a coffee "You'll be needing this then?"

And that was it!

I knew we were going to get

on famously! Not just because Katy knew I liked it milky, but because I came to know that her attention to detail and warm, compassionate personality was unstoppable when it had a focus! And it always had focus: Katy knew exactly how to get results.

Much bigger than the caffeine injection she gave me that day, of course, was Katy's ambition for the *Ten Pieces* Project: an amazing concept with a clear goal - to introduce children to the world of classical music in a way never done before - to inspire them to be creative, as a direct result of the emotion, excitement and wonder of ten very famous pieces of music.

The reaction we have had from thousands of school children all over the UK has been absolutely overwhelming and they have taken their creativity to a whole new level we never imagined.

It has been an absolute pleasure to be a part of Katy's dream and as we continue to present the concerts up and down the country, although hard and with a heavy heart, I remember the 'early days' with fondness and I know Katy would be bursting with pride as the orchestra explodes into action and the children's faces light up at every venue.

This is only the beginning of a journey, a journey that was championed by an incredible woman. Her drive, ambition and indomitable spirit will live on. Not just through the project and those who knew her personally, but through the children's lives and memories, who felt that 'spark' for the first time and who have been inspired.

Katy may not be here anymore but her dreams and energy couldn't be stronger.

And yes, I'm currently sitting in Keele Services. ⊙

Katy Jones

Katy Jones was born and grew up in Dulwich, South London. After attending Brasenose College Oxford, Katy joined Granada Television in 1987, where she worked on 25 *World in Action* programmes. Katy was an active supporter of the Children's Media Foundation, especially in the early days of Save Kids' TV Campaign. She was a firm believer in the benefits of good media and the arts for children and young people and her imagination, tenacity and work ethic were an inspiration.

In 1994 Katy married Mike Spencer, then Head of Granada Television's regional programmes, and they went on to have two children, Huw and Sarah.

Whilst at Granada Television, Katy was appointed Factual Producer, researching Jimmy McGovern's *Hillsborough* (1996). Katy's credits are extensive, from Jimmy McGovern's *Sunday* (2002), *Yasmin* (2004) written by Simon Beaufoy, and Tony Marchant's *Mark of Cain* (2007). In 2011, whilst serving on the Hillsborough Independent Panel, Katy was appointed BBC Learning Zone's Executive Producer, commissioning over 130 educational dramas, documentaries and animations during the following four years. Katy went onto devise the BBC's ambitious *Ten Pieces* project, introducing schoolchildren across the UK to classical music. BBC Director General, Tony Hall, considered it "the biggest commitment the BBC has ever made to music education in our country."

TERRY PRATCHETT 1948-2015

ANN GILES
(BOOKWITCH)

ANN GILES
(BOOKWITCH)

"I'm going to need to interview him." That was the thought going through my head that day shortly after Terry Pratchett received his knighthood. It had dawned on me that he was high up on my interview wish list. Very high up. A witch can but ask, so that's what I did and Terry's publisher Random House didn't actually laugh at me. Or not so I noticed.

Many good stories begin with a librarian, and this one is no different, although the librarian was. Where would we have been without this stern gatekeeper who felt that children should

not be allowed to read any book even vaguely considered as adult? Now that I think of it, I don't suppose she was using reverse psychology on me, the mother of an eleven year old boy? I was quite determined enough – and so was he - that he would read: so no ban on Pratchett was going to come between my child and some of the most wonderful books you could hope to find.

And perhaps there would have been no meetings with Terry, or any buying of Mars bars for him, or trips on steamboats on the Thames in his company, had it not been for a librarian who was more into banning than recommending. If that is the case, then I thank her from the bottom of my heart.

Her, and Neil Gaiman who threw down a gauntlet I couldn't ignore, when he stated Terry was unlikely to be signing any more books.

Ten years on, and I celebrated my son's 21st birthday by interviewing Terry - without the birthday boy - before Terry's platform appearance at the National Theatre to talk about their dramatisation of his children's book *Nation*.

While Clare from Random House fumed over a late running interview with the BBC, I set my stuff up in the small rehearsal room and waited for Terry. Clare brought a jug of water, looked round, and then beat the cushion in the chair I was intending for Terry. I heard his laugh outside in the corridor, and then it was time. "Terry, here is Ann."

"The Bookwitch?"

"That's right."

"Are you a witch in fact?"

"Sort of. Yes. And you're more used to witches than the average author, I believe."

"I have visited concentric circles in my time."

"And she has a broomstick." Clare left to loiter outside and keep track of time.

"Oh, she's gone (he pronounced it 'gorne'), I hope she's going to come back. Something like a Mars bar would actually pick me up at this time... Right, let's go! We've got up until someone comes and gets me. I don't think it's that bad. I think we've clawed some time back."

"When my son was eleven I used to borrow 'adult' audiobooks for his bedtime listening - Agatha Christie, and that sort of thing - from the library, when one day the librarian said I couldn't. Despite me pointing out I was his mother, I was told it wasn't right, and feeling puzzled I asked for an example of something really unsuitable for under-sixteens, and she said 'Terry Pratchett.'"

"What? A librarian actually would... You say *un*suitable?" Terry was flabbergasted.

"Yes, have you ever come across this? Have you been banned anywhere?"

"Oh heavens, please, tell me I have!" His voice rose and he sounded childishly happy. "Actually, the Carnegie medal is, erm, voted for by librarians."

"Yes."

"I think you must have got..."

"... a really bad one?"

"Yes. A really bad 'may-there-be-a-circle-of-hell-for-such-people' librarian. Did you ask her why?"

"I didn't. I was stunned. I'd recently looked round a secondary school library which had a whole shelf of Discworld books."

"I get a lot of letters like 'Dear Sir, We thought our son was dyslexic and he wouldn't read anything at all, and then we gave him Terry Pratchett and he read all the way through Terry Pratchett and now he is professor of comparative philology at the University of Oxbridge'. And I'm not kidding, because I've been around for long enough now that the boys have grown up and have got kids and in some cases grandchildren."

"So you're keen on promoting reading?"

"I would really like to meet a librarian who didn't like my style, and debate with them. I really would!" Terry displayed excitement at the prospect. "I know the books have their heart in the right place. And I know that the books themselves are generally venerated. One critic said that 'at the heart of every Terry Pratchett book you'll find a book'... So Agatha Christie would be OK?"

"Well no, barely."

"Barely OK."

"That's why I asked what would be even worse, and that was you."

"Well, Agatha Christie: you have to get her out of your system sooner or later. Same with James Bond. And then you realise that not all murders happen in one house containing seven people."

"In the library."

Terry laughed. "We looked at a house twenty years ago, in the West Country. We thought of buying an old rectory, which we called the Cluedo house, because it was laid out like that, and it had a secret passage diagonally across. We thought, 'wouldn't it be nice if we got sculptures made of all the [murder weapons], like the lead piping, and put it in each room?'" He laughed merrily.

I asked Terry if he has any child fans, describing an event for a children's book I went to, with only adults.

"Was it for a children's book?"

"Yes, it was *Wintersmith*, and there were about four hundred adults and half a child. I find that your children's books feel more profound than the adult books."

"Yes, I think that tends to be the case. You can actually address issues that you probably wouldn't attempt to address in adult books. There appears to be a kind of freedom, which is fine, but at the same time there are certain shackles. Erm, when you say 'do children read your books?'"

"They obviously do. I think it was more whether they come to events, or whether your children's books are really books for adults?"

"Let's address that one, then. *Nation* won the Printz Award in the States last year, which is the highest Young Adult [YA] book award that you can get if you're not an American. Generally speaking the librarians that vote for this are a tough lot, and the same goes for both my editors, and indeed librarians here." Terry was speaking slowly, clearly thinking how to put it, "they don't want to see an adult book go on the market as a children's book. But there's an interesting, more practical point about that: the gap has narrowed, but traditionally you get a smaller advance for a children's book, irrespective of the size of the book, than for an adult's, so if money was the issue you probably..."

"Then you wouldn't."

"You wouldn't, I think... There appears to be no shortage of fans. I would say that fantasy is uni-age, because at one end of the scale it's got fairy tales, which sometimes are woven into my books. Enough people of all ages are reading enough of my books for me to feel very happy. I never started reading until I was about nine or ten, when I discovered the library, and wanted to read every damned thing. I went not knowing they were sexy novels, but read sexy novels and Tove Jansson and *Just William*. I read anything that I saw, and I think, among children that read, differentiation between 'adult's' and 'children's' gets really quite blurred. Certainly with Discworld, because it looks jolly. And with any luck there's a librarian that will tell you it's not suitable for them," he giggled.

"Can I just say something in passing on that? I'm just on the way to finishing *I Shall Wear Midnight*, which is the last Tiffany Aching, and that is more adult than YA because she grows up. And so there are matters of death. Not matters of sex. And I wondered; there were some things that are very, very scary, in the sense of monsters, and... Have you met Philippa Dickinson?"

"Yes I have."

"Well Philippa knows her stuff, and likewise Anne Hoppe in the States. I occasionally check the boundaries, to be on the safe side. But generally speaking, no matter how fearsome the monster is, the important thing is the fact that that the monster gets defeated."

"That's right."

"The betrayal is if the monster wins. Because Tiffany has had a relationship, which is clearly over, and she thinks kind of bitchy thoughts. She realises she's doing it, but there are little things... Part of the beginning is set on the Discworld version of the Cerne Abbas giant, and there is a bit where you're reading her thoughts. Describing the giant, just saying he had no trousers, is simply just not sufficient to describe his lack of anything... and I thought 'the kids will know exactly what we're talking about.'

I watched my daughter grow up and she was a great kind of marker for me. You know, how she got on with her friends and what they did when they were around the place. It seems to me children are getting older."

At this point Terry was interrupted by the theatre's

publicist, saying we had five minutes left.

"Have we really got five minutes? What I mean is, I don't know how much time there is until I'm now on."

"Forty minutes."

"On the other hand, I've got to have something to eat..."

"Yes."

"So, any more questions you want to ask?"

I mentioned a friend of mine who wrote Terry a fan letter over twenty years ago, asking if he was going to bring Granny Weatherwax back, and in his reply Terry had said no. "She wants to know what made you change your mind."

"That would have been after *Equal Rites*."

"I think so, yes."

"Because when I decided to write *Wyrd Sisters*, I thought, well, Granny Weatherwax is out there, and so, why not? What happens now is quite interesting, with characters that are small in one book, and later on they turn up and we see them in the street or they become the main character. In fact what is 'quite profound' in *I Shall Wear Midnight*, Tiffany goes to Ankh-Morpork and there are a number of people we already know whom she meets. It doesn't matter as far as the kids are concerned, but it feels quite nice.

FAR FAR TOO SOON, OLD FRIEND

"THE WISE MAN SEES DEATH AS A FRIEND" SIR TERRY PRATCHETT

Illustration by Chris Riddell

This is going to be the last Tiffany and it's probably true to say there is not a massive difference between my children's books and my adult books. I mean there is no explicit sex. Never been any good at that sort of thing, you know," Terry said with an embarrassed laugh. "'It's his poor wife that I feel sorry for,'" he muttered under his breath.

"The books go out there and I've always been aware that fantasy is uni-age and the kids who read read anything, and the kids that don't: it's amazing how many you can persuade. Or appear to be persuaded by Discworld."

The door opened again and our time was up, so I quickly whipped out my son's copy of *Good Omens*, asking Terry if he would sign it, "because Neil Gaiman said that there was a space reserved for you."

"Oh, jolly good. Have you got a pen there?"

"Ah, you remember what

you're supposed to write do you?"

"More or less. My handwriting is now so bad. There may be a squiggle there that looks like a signature, let me just double-check." I handed the book back again. "There we are, that fat thing at the bottom which looks like someone's... "

"Thank you."

"Thank you very much. I'm sorry we haven't got longer."

"It's been really good meeting you. Thank you for taking the time."

"Thank you for caring about children's books. You do don't you?"

"I do, but then you write them so well."

"I think that our job is to turn children into adults, not encourage children to remain children."

"A bit like Mau [central character in *Nation*]?'

Terry was halfway out the door, but stopped and considered this; "well, Mau is turned into an adult by force of circumstances. But we're getting into a subject which is not fashionable to talk about." He laughed as he was led off to face the audience in the Olivier, and possibly some food first.

Terry continued on the topic of *Nation* and Mau in his platform talk. It was the story he simply had to write, no matter what it said on the contract for his next book. "This one wrote itself and dragged me after." He felt the adaptation for the stage was fairly good. "You can't have everything but that is nobody's fault. The heart and the soul of the book survived." In some respects Terry thought the theatre version might have been better, since the National had their "props and tricks" to hand, while all Terry had was "one lousy alphabet". And one thing you can't have in a book is a Greek chorus.

The reason Terry set *Nation* in a parallel world, albeit one similar to our own, was that it was his 'get out of jail free' card; he could write whatever he liked without someone pointing out that he got it wrong. He knew exactly what Mau's island was like, having seen it in Australia and even made a model of it in plasticine. Terry said he quite liked islands named after the calendar, with a special fondness for the Mothering Sunday Islands.

While on the subject of dramatisations, Terry reckoned *Wintersmith* would "make a damned good play too." Asked if there might be more books about Johnny [*Johnny and the Dead*; *Johnny and the Bomb*] the reply was "it depends". Terry likened it to a Quaker meeting: you sit in silence until you've got something to say.

Eight months on and Terry hadn't forgotten that our discussion was cut short, so he asked to see me again. Note: Terry Pratchett asked to see me! Obviously, I had to let him, and this time I bundled up not only the missing Mars bar, but my previously sidelined son (to take photos, and to serve coffee and Discworld quotes as and when they were needed).

"You disconcerted me last time by asking 'do children read your books?'"

"Yes, I know."

"Would you like to expand?"

"I reread it and realised it didn't come across terribly clearly. It was more 'do you see them at events?' Last night I saw one boy the right size. When we went to your talk about *Wintersmith* it was just adults, and I thought 'it's a children's book: where are the children?' Or is it only adults who read the books and who come to events?"

"There were lots of kids at the convention, because Discworld cons are very children friendly."

"But are they there because they are children of fans?"

"Ah well, that might be the case. But the point I was going to make is they are like Midwich Cuckoos, because they've been brought up in a house where parents read and venerate books, and they might actually not read Discworld at this point, but they are reading something."

"Yes."

"And when that happens you realise you've scored one for our side. Later this year I'm going to a school where the headmaster has presented every kid with a copy of *Nation*. The whole school has been reading it. I shall also be doing a telephone thing in the States. There they care about teaching about reading rather more than we do. Teachers and librarians seem to have a higher status. I don't think enough British people care enough about what their children read."

"That might be true. If the Americans are different, then I'm glad."

"Well, the Americans who are different, are very different. That doesn't mean there aren't as many uncaring parents but the Americans who care, they try hard. I think I told you about the mother who was reading *The Amazing Maurice* [*and his Educated Rodents*] to her little girl and there was a fraught bit and she was very upset about it. And the daughter wasn't. She patted her mother and said 'don't worry Mum, it will get better by the end.' Because she had a child's belief in narrativium. That of course you have to go through

the horrible dark wood to get to the sunlight at the other side, and that's why you can pull a kid through the dark wood, provided you pull them right out of it. You leave them in the dark wood, the whole book has been wasted."

For *I Shall Wear Midnight*, Terry worried about the contents for young readers. Both his editors told him that a kid who's old enough to read that book will know enough to understand what's happening on the news.

"I had a Mum who talked to me when I was a kid, and told me the stories that her Irish grandma had told her. On the walks to school she told me about things. Sometimes she got them wrong, because of what she could remember about the Greek myths. Talking to kids is important and we don't do it enough any more. Mostly because the parents don't know how to do it.

I think I've told you before, when I was around twelve and thirteen I read every bound copy of the magazine *Punch*. I didn't only look at the humour and the cartoons, I read the other stuff, which had the additional advantage of me picking up a lot of Victorian vocabulary."

This might be a fairly unlikely thing to happen today. Will it deprive future readers? Maybe. Terry's Punch past will have helped him when writing

Dodger, which in turn will give today's children a worthwhile reading experience. I know it did my former eleven year old boy. He might have started with *The Bromeliad*, but *that* librarian notwithstanding he went on to read every single new Terry Pratchett novel, as well as most of the older ones, and in a busy adult world with little time for reading, there has always been time for Terry's books.

And now there is only going to be one more new book: Terry's last gift to us, *The Shepherd's Crown*; his (second) 'last novel' featuring his favourite character, Tiffany Aching. Terry himself has gone to join another of his characters, and I won't be alone in hoping Death is as friendly as he seemed.

Terry Pratchett made reading fun for millions, and he definitely added a lot of pleasure to this witch's life during the five 'interview and book launch' years.

"So where do you come from?"
"Sweden."
"Sweden?"
"Yes."
"Hahaha…"
"It's not that funny."
"Yes, hee hee, it is, it is. Let me tell you a story, to get ourselves warmed up."

Thank you, Terry. It *was* fun.

TERRY SUE-PATT 1964-2015

PHIL REDMOND

When someone younger than you dies there is always that moment of considered mortality. The realisation that death can come at any time. Or, as George Harrison wrote, 'All Things Must Pass'. But when someone passes who had become, whether they realised it or not, whether they wanted it, or liked it or not, a symbol of changing times, the moment is even more poignant.

I didn't know Terry beyond the occasional meetings on the set of *Grange Hill* but, as the obituaries encapsulated, I did know what a symbol Benny Green - the character Terry portrayed - later became. An image of a changing Britain.

The casting credit belongs to Colin Cant, *Grange Hill*'s first Director, who set the style of the programme by reflecting, in both casting and shooting style, the quest for reality that I had set out in the scripts. We both wanted, as far as was possible, kids who could instinctively do real things, rather than be trained to do them as actors.

From the outset, Benny Green had to look like a footballer. Terry was. He had to look like he knew what life was about. Terry did. And he had to have resilience, yet vulnerability to him, to become Tucker Jenkins's sidekick. That too was Terry.

Benny became something else. Something more. The opening face of the programme. Someone had to have that role and it was fitting that it was Terry. And, in 1978, it was not just any face, but a non-white face. From that first kick of the ball on screen, he was destined to become a symbol of *Grange Hill*, its role in a changing Britain as well as the ever-evolving nature of the BBC and its pioneering Children's Department.

No one arrives in any position without interacting with others, and if I wrote Benny, and Colin Cant cast Terry, then credit must also go to Anna Home, Chair of CMF, but then Executive Producer of Drama and later Head of BBC Children's Programmes, for commissioning the programme. Then defending it through all the controversies and antics of Tucker and Benny et al.

Everyone's life has meaning, just as the time for farewell comes to us all. Too often it is difficult to immediately define a life, or point to a moment that changed things for others. Those closer to Terry, beyond the sorrow and sadness, can, hopefully, take some comfort in the fact that in using the football skills that caught Colin Cant's eyes he became the first face seen on *Grange Hill* and, because of that, a symbol of change.

REMEMBERING RENTAGHOST

JEREMY SWAN

An old boom operator came up to me at some do, "Ah, *Rentaghost*!" he said, "We used to love working on that. All those OTT actors standing in a straight line, bawling their lines out front!"

I'd have preferred a more cutting-edge comment on my directorial skills - but at least he did say, "We all loved working on that."

Everyone did. It was the greatest gas.

In North Acton Rehearsal Rooms, rehearsing twelve adults jumping in the air pinching their noses (so they could disappear in a jump cut) needed a LOT of jumping to achieve synchronisation. A weeping

Christopher Biggins hystericked, "I can't believe we're getting paid for this!" Mind you, *Julius Caesar*, rehearsing in the room below, weren't best pleased with the thunderous thumps on their ceiling.

In his autobiography, *Just Biggins*, Christopher writes, "*Rentaghost* wasn't just camp. It was way beyond camp."

I was handed the series by Monica Sims, Head of Children's Programmes, in 1977. Paul Ciani, the original producer, was taking up a position in Singapore. I had directed one episode of *Rentaghost* in Paul's stead the day he had his successful Singaporean interview, so I was a convenient choice to take over the series.

"Do you mind if I make a few changes?" I asked Monica Sims.

"Not at all" - she was the most genial of bosses – then a little stab: "We won't be running it for much longer so make what changes you like."

I did.

The genius behind *Rentaghost* was Bob Block. A writer responsible for *Life with the Lyons*, *Pardon my Genie*, *Robert's Robots*, *Galloping Galaxies!* starring Kenneth Williams, and *Grandad* starring Clive Dunn.

Bob was a dear, bespectacled man and totally above suspicion for the madness, mischief and mayhem that emerged from his pencil. He hand-wrote the scripts and his wife, Madeleine, typed them in camera script format for the convenience of my loyal PAs – Susie Needle, Mary Baxter, Cassie Brabon, Joan Marine and Jillie Sutton. David Crichton directed the film inserts and ran the studio floor. Susie Needle put my credit up as Producer: "You can't do that," I squawked, "I'm not a producer!" "Well, you are now!" she said. So I became the Producer, and the Director, of *Rentaghost*.

Michael Staniforth played Mr Claypole, the jester ghost. During the series he became a West End star of *A Chorus Line*, *Starlight Express* and *Sweeney Todd*. Heavies from Cameron McIntosh's would turn up in the studio to whip him away at six o'clock for the Drury Lane curtain up, so all his scenes had to be shot in time.

Edward Brayshaw played Mr Meaker, the ghosts' manager. Michael Darbyshire was Mr Davenport, a Victorian ghost and Tony Jackson played Fred Mumford, a modern ghost. Betty Alberge and John Dawson played his perplexed living parents. The cast regulars swelled with the arrival of the ghosts' beleaguered neighbours, Mr and Mrs Perkins (Jeffrey Segal and Hal Dyer); Hazel the McWitch (Molly Weir); Adam Painting, a local store owner (Christopher Biggins) and Tamara Novak, a

Nanny ghost (Lynda Marchal).

Lynda was a very talented actress and the audience liked her character – so I wasn't overjoyed when she said she wanted to leave after one series. "Leave?! To do what?" "Write." Lynda Marchal, the very talented actress, left to become Lynda La Plante, the super-talented writer.

The Nanny character was magnificently recast with Sue Nicholls as Nadia Popov. She had a 'little bit' in *Coronation Street* so we had to work around that. The 'little bit' in Corrie is still going strong after nearly 40 years: Sue plays Audrey Roberts.

Kenneth Connor joined as a forgetful ghost, Mr Whatshisname Smith and Aimi MacDonald was Susie Starlight, the ghost of a pantomime fairy.

Bob introduced Mr Claypole's medieval boss – the dreaded Queen Matilda, tyrant of the XII century - played by Paddie O'Neil. She had her entrance in a psychiatrist's office which was being visited by the ghosts' permanently stressed neighbour, Mr Perkins. Whilst prone on the couch, the psychiatrist was sounding him out with his stethoscope. So only Mr Perkins heard the ghostly fanfare. Through the wall, behind the shrink, Queen Matilda processed with her courtiers and out through the opposite wall. Mr

Perkins sat up, gibbering.

"What's the matter?" asked the psychiatrist

He replied: "I've just seen an old queen walking through the wall!"

One series coincided with the release of the movie *The Exorcist*, which scared the pants off cinemagoers in the 1970s. Extremists approached the BBC saying that *Rentaghost* had the potential to make the nation's kids achieve 360 degree head swivelling; emit guttural obscenities; and master projectile vomiting. This, of course, had to be avoided at all costs. Judicious changes of the signature tune were made, omitting words like 'ectoplasm' and changing Mr Claypole's character from a 'poltergeist' to a 'mischievous sprite'.

In a Christmas special, Mr Claypole magicked the Pantomime Horse alive. Dobbin became a regular cast member, gamely played by Bill Perrie in the front and John Asquith in the back, both trained dancers. In one episode, Dobbin, in full tutu, danced the Grand Pas de Deux of Chopin's *Les Sylphides* with a garden gnome in a moonlit idyll. There was nothing sacred in *Rentaghost*!

The four foot high Molly Weir, as Hazel the Mcwitch, wore full witch's garb, including a lethal pointed hat which had the wherewithal to stab out anyone's eye if they got too near, so there were never obscured close-ups of Miss Weir!

Ann Emery (Mrs Meaker – Ethel) has just completed ten years as Billy Elliot's grandma in the Victoria Palace.

We rehearsed the shows Monday to Thursday in North Acton Rehearsal Rooms. On Friday evening we recorded the episode in the Television Centre studio, after camera rehearsal all day. On Saturday I edited and delivered a VHS copy to Jonathan Cohen, the composer, to write the incidental music in a week. He would give me a music tape of the previous week's episode and on Sunday we dubbed all day with a nightmare system called S.Y.P.H.E.R. 'Tired' wasn't in the vocabulary!

The evening recording was planned to go without a hitch. All horrors had been ironed out in the camera rehearsal. The first scene had to include the opening titles and the signature tune; this was preceded by a countdown on the VTR clock. Christopher Biggins farted during one countdown and this reduced him and the cue-awaiting cast to naughty hysterical laughter. They could hardly speak! Molly

Weir had tears cascading down her golden painted face. Sue Nicholls, fully aware of a retake, mimed to her off-camera dresser to get her a cup of tea. Michael Staniforth guffawed all through his lines. The scene ended. I jumped up from my director's chair, yelling, "I'm going down to the floor to murder them!" As I stormed through the adjacent room of lighting and rack operatives, the PA told the Floor Manager via the production mic that, "He's on his way down to murder them." But the lighting and the rack ops were all laughing.

"What's so funny?" I asked.

The Lighting Director answered, "That was. We don't know what they were laughing at but, whatever it was, it made us all laugh too."

I went back to my chair. If it made that lot laugh, the audience would as well.

"Next scene!" I announced into the microphone.

Howls of protest from the cast:

"We were corpsing!"

"I couldn't say my lines!"

"I wet my knickers!"

"It's all Biggins' fault!"

I switched on the tannoy mic:

"Let the audience and your agents see what amateurs you are!!"

AFTERWORD

JOE GODWIN

My first day back to work after Christmas this year was the first day since June 1989 that I hadn't been heading off to do something to do with children's media. This January, after five years as Director of BBC Children's and 26 years in the genre, I'd leapt into a new world, running the BBC Academy and BBC Birmingham. It's been both odd to not be part of the world of children's, and also it's been challenging, learning a whole new set of stuff, people and priorities. It's given the lie to the phrase 'a change is as good as a rest'!

That first day in 1989 was on *Record Breakers* - coincidentally working under producer Greg Childs, now a leading light of The Children's Media Foundation. I think we were filming some 'experts' trying to roll cars over on purpose: apparently there was a world record to be beaten. And then I just stayed: *Going Live*, *Live and Kicking*, *Blue Peter*, Children's Presentation, Nickelodeon, back to the BBC as Head of Entertainment, and finally, Director in 2009, just before we headed up to Salford. (I've missed a few forgettable titles out of this summary.)

Throughout those 26 years, from trainee AP to Director of Children's, so many things have changed (including the risk assessments for filming involving car crashes!): there's the number of TV channels; the inexorable rise of on-demand and YouTube; and the huge move away from studio production skills to self-shot location filming. But as much or more remains the same: the special community of children's media which organisations like the Children's Media Foundation and the Children's Media Conference embody; and the determination of everyone in this genre to produce the highest quality content that focuses on the most discerning audience. And all whilst budgets and schedules have shrunk and new entrants have changed the funding and production models forever.

The other thing that hasn't changed - perhaps surprisingly given all that has - is the standing of the UK children's production and broadcasting industry in the eyes of the world. Wherever I've been in the world talking about children's content, the respect for UK producers and the BBC has not diminished. This is a precious asset I truly hope can continue.

And I hope to continue my connection with UK children's content - as Director of the BBC Academy - helping the BBC and the industry keep ahead of the game on skills and finding the new, diverse talent we need. And also - as Director of BBC Birmingham - thinking how children's genre might play a role in a new Midlands creative industries story.

As many of you know, I've always enjoyed having the last word. And this may be my last last word on the subject of the wonderful world of children's media.

In the Blue Peter garden with former Heads of BBC Children's (from left to right): Nigel Pickard, Lorraine Heggessey, Edward Barnes, Anna Home, Joe Godwin, Dorothy Prior, Richard Deverell, Roy Thompson

CONTRIBUTORS

Lady Rabia Abdul-Hakim

Rabia Abdul-Hakim, affectionately known as 'Lady Rabia', is one the Cayman Islands' most inspiring, personalities: an author, illustrator, speaker, performance poet, master storyteller, playwright, and entrepreneur and real-life heroine.

She has been a lifelong ambassador for the Cayman Islands across various fields including sports, media, arts and culture and gender equality. A corporate diplomat with over a decade of international experience in entrepreneurial and consulting roles, she has worked for high profile clients and organisations in the private and public sectors in the Middle East and in the Cayman Islands.

In 2011, she became a living luminary for single-handedly bringing her six children from the Kingdom of Jordan. Eight months later she launched the Cayman Islands' first culturally-inspired children's media property, *Kaa Kaa & Tokyo*.

The sole hand-drawn cartoonist from the Caymans, the Founding Patron of the BIG Draw KY Family Arts Festival and the host of numerous art and cultural workshops, Lady Rabia was recognized in 2014 with the highest award for creativity: the Cayman National Cultural Foundation (CNCF) Silver Star.

A profound speaker, she has spoken for TEDx and was also commissioned by the Cayman government to creatively address issues like food security and gender equality.

Now living in Stratford-upon-Avon, her company, ContessaBlack Entertainment, develops multicultural children's media. She is a Patron of the CMF and a member of the Society for Storytelling and the Saudi-British Society.

Michael Algar

Michael Algar has worked for fifty years in the film industry. After years of producing TV commercials and sponsored documentaries, he was appointed first Chief Executive of the Irish Film Board in 1982. In that capacity, he supervised the financing of selected feature and documentary films by Irish filmmakers. Also, he represented Ireland on committees in the European Union and the Council of Europe concerning the development and improvement of film industries in Europe.

Since 1989, he has specialised in producing animation both for cinema and television. Credits include the feature, *Christmas Carol*, and series, *The Storykeepers*. He also produced the feature *Joseph,* *King of Dreams*, as well as the series *Teenage Mutant Ninja Turtles*; *Captain Star*; *Budgie the Little Helicopter*; *The Mad Cow*; and many other specials and series. His most recent special was *The Great Fall* and he is currently developing new TV series as well as mobile game apps. He is a member of Animation Ireland, BAFTA and the European Film Academy.

Ken Anderson

Ken is the CEO of Edinburgh based Red Kite group of companies, of which Red Kite Animations, the company he founded, is a part. Other businesses include Red Kite Distribution and the 'light-bulb'-to-screen animation services of Red Kite Studios. Red Kite continually invests in an extensive development slate and is actively looking for new business opportunities within the children's media industries. Shows currently in pre-production include *Bradley and Bee*, with more on the way. Other credits include: *64 Zoo Lane*; *Dennis and Gnasher*; *Ask Lara*; *Wendy*; *Pablo the Little Red Fox*; *The Imp*; *The Secret World of Benjamin Bear*; *Bionicle*; *Wilf the Witch's Dog*. Key areas: Business and Creative Development, International co-production & finance.

Lady Rabia Abdul-Hakim

Michael Algar

Ken Anderson

Daniel Bays

Kerrie-Ann Bernard

Greg Childs

John Chisham

Natalie Coulter

Sophie Edwards

Website:
www.redkite-animation.com

Facebook www.facebook.com/
RedKiteAnimation

LinkedIn: www.linkedin.com/
company/red-kite-animation

Twitter: @redkiteanimatn

Daniel Bays

Passionate about creating outstanding content on all platforms, Daniel Bays created and produced the multi-platform, physically interactive, international hit preschool animated series, *Tree Fu Tom* (for CBeebies and Fremantle Media).

Daniel started his career in creative development - creating shows, brands and formats for BBC Science and Factual Entertainment - and worked up through the ranks of TV production to produce and direct documentaries before moving in to BBC Children's to develop and produce big new ideas, interactive digital experiences and brands (live-action and animation) for all platforms in both CBBC and CBeebies.

Currently Daniel is developing new shows and digital experiences for CBeebies that will hopefully become the next big cross-platform properties.

Kerrie-Ann Bernard

Kerrie-Ann is currently completing an honours degree in communications studies at York University, Canada. Her primary area of interest has been Canadian broadcast policy and children's programming. She has presented papers at conferences at York University and at the Canadian Communication Association at Brock University. Working with Professor Natalie Coulter, Kerrie-Ann is currently completing a thesis paper focusing on the unique use of interstitial content by Kids' CBC to broadcast distinctly Canadian content to a children's audience.

Greg Childs

Greg was a director, producer and executive producer of children's programmes at the BBC, where he also created the first BBC children's websites and developed and launched the children's channels CBBC and CBeebies and their interactive services. From 2004, Greg advised many companies on their cross-media strategies. He also worked on the launch of Teachers TV and the CITV channel, and spent three years as a consultant to Al Jazeera Children's. Greg is currently Head of Studies (Interactive and Transmedia) at the German Akademie Für Kindermedien; Editorial Director of the Children's Media Conference; and Director of the Children's Media Foundation. Greg is a Fellow of the RSA and a BAFTA member.

John Chisham

My name is John Chisham. I am a living/ functioning teenage schoolboy from Cambridge, who enjoys writing and is in a band. I have written numerous plays, songs and stories; particular favourites include my farcical comedy 'The Widows Club', my Shakespeare parody 'Forbantzio', my physical theatre piece 'Chefs on the Titanic' and material for my indie rock band 'Kermode Sprit'. I am currently studying Drama, Media Studies and English Literature at A Levels. I've also been in a Branston Pickle advert, which is always an excellent icebreaker. I like spending time with my family - mum, dad and two younger sisters - as well as my friends. Also, as you'd expect from your everyday friendly neighbourhood teenager I enjoy watching TV and sleeping. Following college, I shall be studying drama at university, as well as washing my own clothes,which genuinely scares me. After university I plan to pursue a career in the creative industries as a writer and/or actor.

Natalie Coulter

Natalie Coulter is currently an Assistant Professor at York

Jenny Ehren

Ann Giles

Joe Godwin

Stuart Harrison

Barney Harwood

Beth Hewitt

Jon Howard

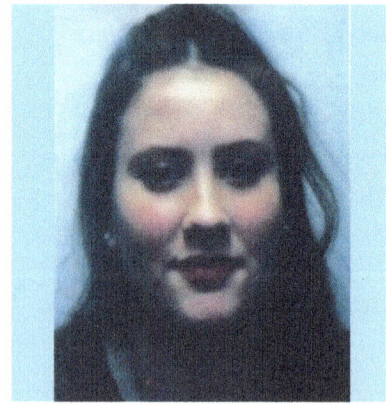

Josie Kelly

Sachiko Kodaira

University in the department of Communication Studies. Her research interests are in girls' studies, critical advertising studies and the media of children and young people. Her book *Tweening the Girl: The Crystallization of the Tween Market* has been published by Peter Lang's Mediated Youth series. She has published in the *Canadian Journal of Communication*, *Jeunesse* and *Popular Communication*. She is a founding member of ARCYP (Association for Research on the Cultures of Young People). She presently has two research projects underway, one of the history of children's cultural industries in Canada; and another on the embodied tween: living girlhood in global and digital spaces.

Sophie Edwards

Sophie Edwards lives in Manchester, she is a year nine student and is about to begin her GCSEs. She enjoys art, sports, and plays netball for her school team. She hopes to pursue a career in the arts. Outside of school she enjoys meeting up with friends, baking and going to the cinema.

Jenny Ehren

Jenny Ehren has been a children's researcher for ten years. Her work covers all aspects of children's lives, and across the age range from preschool to college and university. She focuses on qualitative research techniques for the most part, consulting primarily with children but also with the adults involved in their lives, such as parents, teachers and other youth professionals. Her key areas of interest are media use and behaviour; education and careers; and social issues concerning and relating to young people.

She is also closely involved in the regular programme of published research at CHILDWISE. She is lead researcher for the annual Preschool Report which establishes key behaviour patterns among preschool children, and she contributes to the annual CHILDWISE Monitor Report which tracks children's media use and purchasing behaviour.

Jenny has two young children, one at nursery and one at primary school. She is a member of the Market Research Society and the Association of Qualitative Researchers.

Ann Giles

Ann Giles is senior writer at Bookwitch. In fact she is the only one there, apart from when she invites the great and the famous from the children's book world to contribute.

After a degree in English and Swedish from the University of Gothenburg, Ann married her husband (quite a coincidence) and moved to the UK where she did very little until her two children arrived and forced some activity from her, as well as re-introducing children's books into her life for the third time.

The children grew, and so did her preoccupation with books, until 2007 when she sprung into complete Bookwitch mode and finally had a genuine reason for bothering authors and asking for free books. Her heroes are surprisingly willing to be interviewed and to do things for her.

Bookwitching is a full time hobby that brings in no money. Quite the reverse, mostly. Some adult crime has found its way into this children's books area, and Ann has a special interest in fiction and non-fiction in relation to autism. There is also CultureWitch for films, television and anything else vaguely cultured, and occasionally the Swedish Bookwitch sticks her head above the parapet when she has something to say.

Do contact Ann (via the Bookwitch site) if you are able to introduce her to J K Rowling,

Cat Lewis

Russell Miller

Megan Nicholson

Simon Parsons

Alison Preston

Phil Redmond

Chris Riddell

Andy Robertson

Angela Salt

but please don't send any more Harry Potter clones.

https://bookwitch.wordpress.com

Joe Godwin

Joe is Director of the BBC Academy, the UK media sector's biggest skills trainer. He is also head of centre for BBC Birmingham. As Director of the BBC Academy, Joe is responsible for putting training and development at the heart of the BBC. As Director of BBC Birmingham, he's responsible for pan-Birmingham BBC initiatives, developing external partnerships, and the overall leadership of the Birmingham sites. Previously, Joe was Director of BBC Children's, responsible for all of the BBC's services for children on CBBC and CBeebies.

After reading History at Manchester University, Joe joined the BBC in 1986, working at BBC Southampton in regional news. In 1989 he joined the Children's Programmes department as a trainee, and worked as an assistant producer, studio director and producer on shows such as *Blue Peter, Going Live and Record Breakers*. From 1997 to 2000 he was Editor of Children's Presentation. In 2000 he moved to Nickelodeon UK, holding a number of posts including Head of Original Production and VP Interactive Director. Joe returned to the BBC in 2005 as Head of Children's Entertainment, and in 2008 became Head of News, Factual & Entertainment.

Joe is a member of the Advisory Panel on Children's Viewing of the British Board of Film Classification.

Stuart Harrison

Stuart Harrison is an award-winning character designer and cartoon illustrator with over twenty years of experience across children's media and the communication design industries. He established Fun Crew in 2006 with his wife, writer Angela Salt. Together they create original and marketable properties and children's content with an emphasis on animated comedy, strong storytelling and great characters!

Fun Crew are currently developing *Bear, Bud & Boo*, an adorable animated comedy with global partners, Technicolor, for children aged 4–7.

Stuart and Angela have three children aged sixteen, thirteen and eight. Stuart has a bigger toy collection (vintage TOMY robots, urban vinyl and Star Wars) than all three put together...

Barney Harwood

Barney has always been a keen entertainer and made his first television appearance at just two years old when he was interviewed by a local TV station. His first love is music; he has been playing the piano and guitar since the age of six, so naturally decided to pursue this as a career as soon as he could. When he was seventeen years old, he sent a tape to Take That manager Nigel Martin Smith, who spotted potential in Barney and signed him up for his latest project as part of a boy band called Goal who then went on to appear on television shows such as *Children's Ward* and then a tour of the UK as part of the Mizz Road show of '98.

Barney turned his hand to acting, filming extra work for *Hollyoaks, Brookside, Coronation Street* and *Cold Feet* which eventually led to him landing a role alongside Frank Skinner in the sitcom *Heavy Reavie*. Barney then went on to present a digital TV show known as *Whereits.at*, which was broadcast live from the Trocadero centre in London's West End, it was here where he developed his skills in live television presenting.

In 2001 BBC Bosses asked him to join the team at CBBC, where he has been entertaining

Peter Saunders

Jeanette Steemers

Jeremy Swan

Alice Webb

Agnieszka Weglinska

Helen Wheatley

Lynn Whitaker

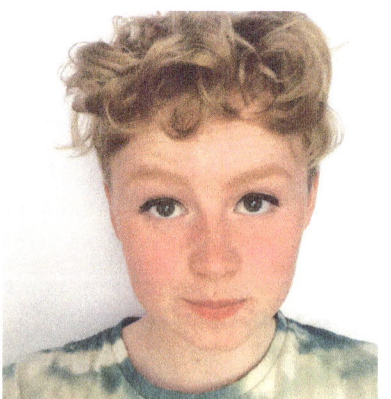

Flora Wilson Brown

Ruth Zanker

the nation's children ever since. Over his thirteen years at the BBC, Barney has become a popular face: initially through his work on the flagship Sunday morning show *Smile* alongside his friend, Nev the bear. Barney was awarded a BAFTA for best TV presenter after spending six years there. He also won Best Script and Best One Off Film at the Kidscreen awards in New York for the *Newsround Special – Gone*. More recently, he presented another special on Alcohol which was also awarded a BAFTA.

Many children recognise Barney from *Bear Behaving Badly* where he stars alongside Nev the Bear and Mr Angry Pants, here Barney established himself as a natural comedy actor in a lead role for the BBC. Barney also wrote the theme tune and music for the show.

As well as a string of successful shows such as *Crush*; *Totally Doctor Who*; *Sorcerer's Apprentice*; *Smokehouse*; *Barney's Barrier Reef*; *Barney's Latin America*; *Natural Born Hunters*; *Silent School*; *Smile*; *Basil & Barney's Swap Shop*; *Bear Behaving Badly*; and the extremely popular *Prank Patrol* (which he also wrote music for), Barney presented the BBC Proms at the Royal Albert Hall alongside Sir David

Attenborough with whom he filmed the children's series of *Inside Life*.

Barney joined the BBC's flagship children's show *Blue Peter* in January 2010 and is still proud to be sailing on board what he says is "the best boat in kids telly".

Beth Hewitt

Salford International Media Festival Director Beth Hewitt is also Director of Conversion for the School of Arts and Media, and Programme Leader in MA Children's Digital Media, at the University of Salford.

Beth's love of the media industry began with two weeks work experience at Cosgrove Hall Productions. After three years at University of Warwick, she got her first job in the industry at Granada ITV where she went onto research, direct and produce arts programmes and factual documentaries. She went onto produce and direct for BBC Factual Entertainment.

Beth then moved to the National Media Museum as producer within the Learning Department, followed by two years at Urbis in Manchester, creating projects and bringing media industry practitioners and young people together. Whilst at Urbis, she also became co-director of Exposures Moving

Image Festival in collaboration with Cornerhouse (now HOME). Beth sits on the Royal Television Society (North West) Committee panel, producing and supporting events.

Beth moved to University of Salford in 2008 as Senior Lecturer in Media Practice, where she led the MA Documentary programme and went on to write the MA Media Production: Children's Television Production programme, which she currently leads.

@bethhewitt1

BestFest13 - Instagram

Jon Howard

Jon is an Executive Product Manager for BBC Digital, working closely with BBC Children's and youth brands to deliver interactive experiences. This role entails developing and delivering audience focused products that deliver strategic value to the BBC. The process involves working alongside Interactive/TV producers, User Experience experts, the BBC Research and Development department and many of the world's best digital agencies.

Jon had a lead role in the massively successful CBeebies 'Playtime' app and over the years has designed, developed and lead on hugely successful games for major UK and international kid's brands - including *Doctor Who; Scooby Doo; Tree Fu Tom; Rastamouse; Shaun the Sheep; Charlie & Lola; Dick & Dom; Horrible Histories; Escape from Scorpion Island*; and many more.

Jon takes a keen interest in creativity, innovation, and technology advancements: he is a creative coder, a prolific game-maker, a speaker at international conferences and an enthusiastic mathematician/statistician - with a great passion for BBC Children's, digital media and interactive experiences.

Josie Kelly

I am an eighteen year old A level student who has a life plan but no idea how to get there. I have a passion for left wing politics and more or less anything else that you can paint a protest poster for. I love cats and have a pure hatred for writing essays and anything with six or more legs. I love debating and arguing and always seem to come across the most obnoxious and arrogant people who need to be told they are wrong. I'm also very sarcastic.

Sachiko Kodaira

Since joining NHK (Japan Broadcasting Corporation), Japan's only public broadcaster, in 1977, Sachiko Imaizumi

Kodaira has been conducting various kinds of studies regarding children and media and the educational use of media at the NHK Broadcasting Culture Research Institute. She studies both the Japanese situation and international trends. She also served as an educational affairs commentator on NHK Radio and TV 2000–2009. In 2006, she served as a Jury member for the JAPAN PRIZE, which is an international contest for educational media started in 1965 by NHK.

She is a member of the Japan Association for Educational Media Study [Vice President, 2009-2015], the Japan Society for Studies in Journalism and Mass Communication [Board member, 1997-2001] and the Japan Society for Educational Technology. She has taught on a part time basis at Sophia University (Tokyo), Osaka University, The Open University of Japan, and more.

Her recent publications available in English via her website include 'Trends in World Educational Media: Based on Entries to the JAPAN PRIZE since 2000' (2011); 'Advancing Digitalization in Japanese Classrooms and the Future of Media Use in Education: From the 2010 NHK School Broadcast Utilization Survey' (2011);

'Children's Television: Trends around the World' (2005); and 'Where does educational TV go?' (2005).

Cat Lewis

Cat is a BAFTA and Royal Television Society award-winning Executive Producer, who runs her own Manchester based independent, Nine Lives Media, employing between 20 and 40 programme makers at any one time. The company makes documentaries, children's programmes, current affairs, factual formats and drama documentaries for BBC One, Channel 4, Channel 5, BBC Three, CBBC, C&I Network and TLC (The Learning Channel in USA).

Nine Lives recently created one of the highest rating new factual series on any channel. BBC One's *Pound Shop Wars* attracted a consolidated audience of 7 million and has won critical acclaim.

Nine Lives made the first ever programme about a transgender child to be commissioned by CBBC – 'I Am Leo' – and the BAFTA winning film 'Me, My Dad & His Kidney' as well as 'The Burns Club', 'One Way Ticket' and is in production with 'Walking with Elephants' for *My Life*.

The company is a regular

supplier to BBC Current Affairs and one of just three UK independent production companies with an output deal for Channel 4's *Dispatches*.

Cat has been on TV's trade association PACT's national Council for four years and is its former Vice Chair. She is also Chair of PACT's Nations & Regions Committee. Nine Lives is the Manchester partner member of the Creative Industries Foundation; Cat is the founder and chair of the North's Indie Club; is Vice Chair of Creative Skillset's TV Panel; is on the North's Creative Skillset Panel and is on the RTS Committee in the North West.

Russell Miller

Over the course of more than three decades, Russell Miller has created electronic, print, live and transmedia properties for clients from Sesame Workshop, Disney and PBS stations, to the Metropolitan Opera. He was the first - and only - director of education at Noggin and The N, Nickelodeon's educational channels for preschoolers and young adolescents. He's now CEO/Founder of WONDERREEL©: the first online video/social platform designed especially for 6-11 year olds, streaming quality children's entertainment from all over the globe to any digital device. (Learn more at www. planetwonderreel.pw.)

A writer and filmmaker, Miller has reported for *The New York Times*, *Los Angeles Times*, *Rolling Stone*, *GQ*, *Life* and New York Public Radio; he's written documentary films for Turner Network Television, the American Film Institute, and the Juilliard School of Music. He has taught on the politics and ethics of communications (Hunter and Baruch Colleges, City University of New York), child development (Queens College, CUNY), and journalism for children (Radcliffe College, Harvard University). Trained as a developmental psychologist, Miller also conducts research on the psychometrics of cognition at the Graduate Center, City University of New York.

Megan Nicholson

Megan Nicholson is nearing the end of her Master's degree in Children's Television Production at the University of Salford. Upon graduating, she wants to take on the role of a junior researcher within an independent production company, based in London.

She says that, although The University of Salford's building at MediaCityUK, has been the best environment for herself and her peers to develop this year (in skills such as scriptwriting; casting; camera work; production management; directing; and editing), she would like to explore more of the independent side to television production in the big city.

Megan is a keen researcher: she has worked with young children and studied media audiences and theories since A Level. She also has a very varied taste in music, film, and TV, and loves extreme sports, and being in the outdoors. Her passion for children's storytelling began as a youngster and has stayed with her throughout her career.

Megan has been involved in the running of local children's book festivals, she has partaken in 4Talent Days, volunteered at the UK's largest Documentary Film Festival, Sheffield Doc Fest, as well as being a regular volunteer for the Children's Media Conference.

Simon Parsons

Simon is an Amnesty International award-winning filmmaker with 29 years of broadcast experience and the former head of BBC Children's in Scotland. It was in 1997 that he began making programmes for the children's audience. He quickly rose through the ranks to become executive producer of *Live and Kicking* and the *Saturday Show* broadcast live for three hours every Saturday on BBC One. In 2005 he joined the network board of BBC Children's and became head of children's production for the BBC in Scotland. While he was in charge, the department produced a fifth of the BBC's network children's television programmes and won three BAFTAs.

Alongside departmental success Simon had a personal triumph winning an Amnesty International Media Award as producer of a documentary about asylum seeker children, called the *Glasgow Girls*. As well as producing *Teacup Travels* he is now writing fiction for 8-12 year olds and a nonfiction book about modern childhood titled *Remember the Kindness of Strangers*.

Alison Preston

Alison Preston is head of media literacy research at Ofcom, the independent regulator and competition authority for the UK communications industries.

She leads Ofcom's media literacy research, which provide a wealth of data on the media habits and opinions of children aged 5–15 and their parents, and adults aged 16+, interviewing over 6,000 people annually. Its *Media use and attitudes* reports show trends since 2005 in the areas of take-up and use of different media, with a particular focus on internet habits and attitudes.

She joined Ofcom in 2003, and previously worked as a research consultant in digital media policy and independent TV production business models. She has a doctorate from the University of Stirling which examined the development of the UK's TV news industry, and has carried out a number of multi-country analyses of TV news coverage of conflicts.

Phil Redmond

Phil Redmond was awarded his CBE in 2003 for 'Services to Drama', as a consequence of his innovatory television career at Mersey Television that included *Grange Hill, Brookside* and *Hollyoaks*. Many went on from Mersey Television to forge distinguished careers in their own right.

Alongside this career, Phil, together with his wife Alexis, also supports many charitable and public sector causes becoming major benefactors across Merseyside, including Liverpool John Moores University, National Museums Liverpool and Alder Hey Hospital.

Since he and Alexis sold Mersey Television in 2005, Phil has devoted almost all of his time to public service including taking the high profile public role of Deputy Chair and Creative Director of Liverpool's year as European Capital of Culture 2008, which many have said would not have had such a positive effect on Liverpool's renaissance without his involvement. Phil has also chaired the Merseyside Entrepreneurship Commission and the Knowsley Youth Commission.

As well as continuing local charity work across Merseyside and Cheshire, Phil is Chair of: National Museums Liverpool; The Institute of Cultural Capital, a joint initiative between Liverpool John Moores University and the University of Liverpool; Liverpool's Mayoral Commission on Creativity; and The Independent Advisory Panel to the UK City of Culture programme that awarded the title to Derry-Londonderry in 2013 and Hull for 2017.

Chris Riddell

Chris Riddell studied at the Epsom School of Art and Design and was a student of Raymond Briggs at Brighton Polytechnic. As well as working as a political cartoonist for *The Economist, The Independent* and *The Observer*, Chris has

created an extraordinary range of books which have won many illustration awards including the UNESCO Prize and the Greenaway Medal (twice). These include the highly-acclaimed Ottoline titles and the 2013 Costa Children's Book Award-winning *Goth Girl* and the *Ghost of a Mouse*. Chris has also achieved international success through his best-selling collaboration with Paul Stewart (*The Edge Chronicles*) and through his illustrated works for other high-profile figures including Neil Gaiman and the comedian Russell Brand.
As an artist and illustrator in command of a variety of forms and genres, ranging from political satire to picture books, graphic novels to crossover fantasy, Chris Riddell demonstrates a broad understanding of visual communication for all ages. He has also been celebrated for his inclusion of themes of 'otherness' and of tolerance to a young audience without ever becoming didactic or pedantic. Coupled with his classical drawing ability, Riddell has earned the respect and adoration of diverse audiences across several generations. He is currently occupying the post of the Booktrust Writer in Residence. He lives and works in Brighton. He has just been appointed as the new Waterstones Children's Laureate for 2015-2017.

Andy Robertson

Andy Robertson has three children aged seven, ten and twelve. He is a freelance journalist specialising in family technology. He writes for national newspapers and appears on broadcast TV as a family gaming expert and runs the YouTube channel 'Family Gamer TV'.

Drawing on a theological training, his perspective of games as potentially meaningful and culturally significant experiences led to a TEDx talk; a video-game led service in Exeter Cathedral; and exhibiting games at schools and arts festivals.

Angela Salt

Angela Salt is a writer, creative producer and co-owner of Fun Crew, an independent children's content creation studio she founded with her husband, Stuart Harrison, in 2006. They have three children aged sixteen, thirteen and eight and live by the seaside in Southport.

Angela is a keen advocate of the CMC and UK@Kidscreen and encourages other small, independent creative companies to join the industry. Prior to starting Fun Crew she worked as a successful editorial illustrator and educator tutoring in illustration, ideas generation and development, and art direction for advertising and communication media design at Kingston, Manchester Metropolitan and Salford Universities and The School Of Communication Arts in London. She draws on her visual arts background when creating new ideas for children adding great characters, imaginative storytelling and fun ideas! As a writer she's worked in comics, publishing and comedy. She's the author of three books for Scholastic.

Fun Crew are currently developing an adorable animated comedy, *Bear, Bud & Boo*, with Technicolor, which Angela originally created and is currently writing.

Peter Saunders

Peter Saunders studied animation before developing his puppet making skills on Jim Henson's feature film *The Dark Crystal* in the early 1980s. He later learned to adapt and miniaturise animatronic mechanisms, which enabled him to create highly sophisticated stop-motion puppets at Cosgrove Hall Productions. He was joined at the studio by Ian Mackinnon and together they pioneered new techniques in the art of puppet making on productions such as BAFTA-winner *The Reluctant Dragon* and Emmy Award-winner *The Fool of the World*.

At the start of the 1990s, Peter and Ian left Cosgrove Hall and set up their business partnership. Over the last twenty years, Mackinnon & Saunders have received commercial and critical acclaim for their contributions to an impressive number of feature films, shorts films, TV series and specials. They have worked on many children's TV shows including *Wind In the Willows*; *Postman Pat*; *Bob the Builder*; *Pingu*; *Strange Hill High*; *Rastamouse*; *Raa Raa the Noisy Lion*; and the new *Clangers*, and created the puppet characters for Wes Anderson's *Fantastic Mr Fox*, Tim Burton's *Mars Attacks!*, *Corpse Bride* and *Frankenweenie*. In 2013, the company launched a new digital animation venture – Mackinnon & Saunders Digital Studios – which produced *Wanda & the Alien*, a kids' series for Channel 5/Nickelodeon.

In 1989, Peter took a year-long break to sail from England to the Red Sea and back with his wife Ellen. On their return to the UK, Peter and Ellen founded and ran a charity called The Turtle Fund, helping to protect loggerhead turtles in the Mediterranean.

Peter has two grown-up children and his interests include history, reading, sailing and tinkering about on a vintage WW2 Willys Jeep.

Jeanette Steemers

Professor Jeanette Steemers is Co-Director of the Communications and Media Research Institute (CAMRI) at the University of Westminster. A graduate in German and Russian at the University of Bath, she completed her PhD in 1990, on public service broadcasting in West Germany. After working for research company, CIT Research, and international television distributor HIT Entertainment, she rejoined academia in 1993. Her book publications include *Changing Channels: The Prospects for Television in a Digital World* (1998); *Selling Television: British Television in the Global Marketplace* (2004); *European Television Industries* (2005 together with P. Iosifides and M. Wheeler); *Creating Preschool Television* (Palgrave); *The Media and the State* (in press with T. Flew and P. Iosifidis); and *European Media in Crisis* (in press with J. Trappel and B. Thomass). She has published widely on UK television exports and the children's media industry. Her work has been funded by the British Academy, the Leverhulme Trust and the AHRC. She is currently working on a three year AHRC funded project on 'Orientations in the Development of Pan-Arab Television for Children' with Professor Naomi Sakr.

Jeremy Swan

Jeremy Swan started his career in the Dublin Gate Theatre as a child actor, playing the page in a European tour of Shaw's *Saint Joan*. He subsequently worked as a designer, then moved onto Ardmore Studios in Co. Wicklow where he watched movie magic as the fifth assistant director on *The Spy Who Came in From the Cold*. He joined RTE when it started in 1960, and in 1966 went to work for Granada armed with a recipe for paella and a Spanish dictionary: leaving-Ireland presents from his granny. He went from floor managing *Coronation Street* to the BBC where he became a producer in Children's Programmes. After a time as a director on *Jackanory*, he inherited a programme called *Rentaghost*, written by Bob Block, giving Jeremy, a troop of mad actors, and – luckily - the audience, a terrific time! Bob then put his pen to a series for Clive Dunn as *Grandad*. And that packed even more hilarity into everyone's lives. Jeremy went from the BBC to TVS to direct *Fraggle Rock* for the Jim Henson Organisation, and, on returning to the BBC, Anna Home, Head of Children's Programmes, sent him to Melbourne to work on *Round the Twist* for the Australian Children's Foundation. Sooty invited him to direct him, Sweep and Soo for ITV. He current works as a painter (pictures, not walls) and as a playwright, based in London.

Alice Webb

Alice Webb is the Director of BBC Children's, the world's leading public service broadcaster for children and home of the UK's two most popular networks for kids - CBeebies and CBBC.

BBC Children's is the biggest investor in British-made content and serves its audience with connected, multi-platform experiences based in the form of shows, games and apps based on their favourite characters and brands. These include the BAFTA-winning *Katie Morag; The Dumping Ground; Justin's House; Wolfblood; Blue Peter; Newsround; Mr Bloom's Nursery; The Furchester Hotel; Horrible Histories*; and many, many more.

Alice is hugely proud to be part of BBC Children's and looks forward to continuing its unique purpose and pioneering tradition. She wants BBC Children's to be a driving force in helping to shape the rapidly-evolving digital world today's kids are growing up in, so that they can learn, thrive, have fun and realise their full potential. Her three kids are pretty thrilled too (but for slightly different reasons).

Alice took up this role in March 2015, after spending six years as Chief Operating Officer (COO) for BBC North and BBC England. One of her proudest achievements to date is orchestrating the move of BBC departments including Sport, Children's, 5 live and Learning to Salford. Since this relocation, programme-makers in BBC North have helped deliver a fully Digital Olympics and Commonwealth Games, award-wining programmes including *Last Tango in Halifax* and *Happy Valley*, and number one apps including CBeebies 'Playtime' and 'Storytime'.

Alice is a Trustee of the Greater Manchester Art Centre (Home) and is a member of the Greater Manchester Business Leadership Council.

Agnieszka Weglinska

Agnieszka Weglinska is a senior lecturer in the Department of Journalism and Communication, The Faculty of Social Science and Journalism at the University of Lower Silesia in Wroclaw - Poland. Agnieszka's research concentrates on public service media, new media and transformation of media systems in Europe. She has written many articles on policy and social issues affecting public service media. Her most recent books (as editor) are *Internet television and the borderlines of post-television media* (2013), *Social transformation in Poland – European context – modernity, media and material culture* (2015). She is a member of The Polish Communication Association. Agnieszka is a trainer in the field of children's media content at The University of the Third Age.

Helen Wheatley

Helen Wheatley is Associate Professor in Film and Television Studies at the University of Warwick. She is a member of the Department of Film and Television Studies and the Centre for Television History, Heritage and Memory Studies. She has research interests in various aspects of British television history, and has published work on popular genres in television drama in the UK, US, including the monograph *Gothic Television* (2006). She has ongoing interests in issues of television history and historiography, the topic of her edited collection *Reviewing Television History: Critical Issues in Television Historiography* (IB Tauris, 2007). Her next book is *Spectacular Television: Exploring Televisual Pleasure* (IB Tauris, 2016). She is also developing a research project with her colleague Dr. Rachel Moseley on the history of children's television culture in Britain which is the subject of a large-scale touring exhibition, 'The Story of Children's Television from 1946 to Today' on which they have collaborated with colleagues at the Herbert Art Gallery and Museum, Coventry.

Lynn Whitaker

Lynn is a lecturer in cultural policy and cultural industries at the Centre for Cultural Policy Research, University of Glasgow, and her research straddles all aspects of media production from policy through to audience. Her PhD was a production study of BBC Scotland children's department and she is Editor of the *Children's Media Yearbook*. Lynn's current research is into children's in-app purchasing, and she is interested in developing further knowledge exchange with creative industries. She is a Fellow of the RSA and a trustee of the VLV. Lynn is a

keen swimmer – she recently completed a 5k - and enjoys ballroom and Latin dancing. She lives in Glasgow with her husband and teenage son as well as a cat and a (surprisingly fast) tortoise. She won the CMC dance-off in 2014!

Flora Wilson Brown

I'm Flora, I'm eighteen and I'm currently studying for my final A Level exams in History, English Literature and Theatre Studies at Hills Road Sixth Form College. Since joining Hills I've been increasingly involved in the Drama department there: acting and assistant directing in staff productions and even having two of my own plays performed (*Capital R*, focusing on the prison system and how we treat criminals as a society, and *Bea and April*, following a journey of friendship). I've also been lucky enough to take part in some Young Writers' workshops with Menagerie Theatre and hope to pursue playwriting after leaving Hills. That said, I have really enjoyed writing a reflective piece for this yearbook, on the internet and its peculiar effects on my generation in particular: something I'm fascinated by and am now considering mining in my future writing, having been given this opportunity to consider it in detail.

Ruth Zanker

I am part of the research team at the New Zealand Broadcasting School in Christchurch New Zealand. My research relates to the New Zealand media ecology and how it relates to the global context. I have a particular interest in children's media rights and the way current provision improves or impedes access for them to local media diversity and media production opportunities. I was founding chair of The Children's Television Foundation which successfully fought for national public funding for children's content under the Broadcasting Act of 1989. This dedicated fund is disbursed to free to air broadcasters, after a competitive proposal round, by New Zealand On Air. I am currently a trustee on the New Zealand Children's Screen Trust (kidsonscreen.co.nz) which is working with New Zealand On Air to scope a digital strategy for children's delivery. This will be finalized in 2016. In 2014, I was a judge for the Prix Jeunesse awards. In 2006 I created Mediascape, designed to share information, research and opinion between diverse media stakeholders in New Zealand. The website was archived in 2011, not because of lack of users, but due to earthquakes and lack of funding.

Lightning Source UK Ltd.
Milton Keynes UK
UKOW07f0742260615

254173UK00003B/13/P

9 780957 551848